The Deuce Coupe that Stole My Heart

A Memoir about Building a Hot Rod

Richard Stoebel

THE DEUCE COUPE THAT STOLE MY HEART: A Memoir About Building a Hot Rod
Copyright © 2022   Richard Stoebel All rights reserved.

All rights reserved. No part of this book may be reproduced or used in any manner without written permission of the copyright owner except for the use of quotations in a book review.

Cover Design, Typography, & Production by Hallard Press LLC
Cover Image: William Mitchell

Published by Hallard Press LLC.
www.HallardPress.com   Info@HallardPress.com   352-234-6099
Bulk copies of this book can be ordered at Info@HallardPress.com

Publisher's Cataloging-in-Publication data

Names: Stoebel, Richard, author.
Title: The deuce coupe that stole my heart: a memoir about building a hot rod / Richard Stoebel.
Description: The Villages, FL: Hallard Press LLC, 2022.
Identifiers: LCCN: 2022912573 | ISBN: 978-1-951188-60-3 (paperback) | 978-1-951188-61-0 (ebook)
Subjects: LCSH Stoebel, Richard. | Automobiles--Conservation and restoration. | Automobiles--United States--History--20th century. | Ford automobile--Conservation and restoration. | BISAC BIOGRAPHY & AUTOBIOGRAPHY / Personal Memoirs | TRANSPORTATION / Automotive / Antique & Classic
Classification: LCC TL152.2 .S76 2022 | DDC 629.2222/092--dc23

Printed in the United States of America   1

ISBN: (Paperback) 978-1-951188-60-3

ISBN: (Ebook) 978-1-951188-61-0

Dedication

To my wife, Brenda, who makes all things possible in married life.
Thank you for allowing me the resources and time to write another book and to fulfill a newly discovered passion.

CHAPTER 1

My love of cars began at a very young age.

My first recollection of driving any kind of vehicle was when I was about six or seven years old. My parents took my sister and me to Whalom Amusement Park in Lunenburg, Massachusetts. The park was established in 1893 as an English garden and grew over the years to include a roller coaster and a merry-go-round. The park was closed and abandoned in 2000 after a 107-year run. Back in the early 1950s, Whalom Amusement Park was a big attraction. One of the rides that caught my attention was a road course where you could drive individual cars around a track. The cars were not like go-carts of today, but resembled miniature Model T Fords. The road course was lined with sideboards about a foot high so you could not leave the track even if you drove into them. I must have met the age and height requirement to drive the course because, before I knew it, I was behind the wheel of one of the cars.

I can still remember to this day completing the entire ride without hitting any of the sideboards. I felt it was a huge accomplishment and I was proud to tell my parents and anyone else who would listen how well I drove. From that day forward, I knew I was going to enjoy a lifetime of driving anything with wheels, whether it was bicycles, motorcycles, cars, golf carts, farm equipment, or hot rods. Driving would be one of the pleasures in my life. I just knew it.

I think anyone, especially boys, took pride in identifying any car that passed by. In the mid-1950s, cars were easy to identify because, from year to year, car manufacturers made body changes that were easily recognizable. For instance, it was easy to spot a 1957 Chevy or a 1958 Chevy. Even though there were different models within a particular year—like a convertible, station wagon, coupe or sedan, the distinctive features of the body always stood out. You could easily recognize the rear quarter panel of a 1957 or 1958 Chevy because of its unique styling.

As I entered my teenage years, I got a job at a local apple orchard in Bolton, Massachusetts. Kids could pick dropped apples for 15 cents a bushel. Drops, as they were referred to, were apples that either fell naturally off the tree, or fell as workers were picking the fruit from ladders. These apples could not be sold to the public so they were sent to the cider mill. This was my first job, and I earned a few dollars a week in the fall. My mother was the financial head of our

The Deuce Coupe that Stole My Heart

1957 Chevrolet with distinctive rear quarter panels and probably best known and loved of the 1950's Chevrolets.

1958 Chevrolet with different rear quarter panel styling. While not as iconic as the 1957 Chevy, still easily recognizable.

family, so she made sure I paid a little "room and board" to the household, kept a little for personal spending, and the rest was put into a savings account.

The next year, I graduated to picking apples from a ladder for 25 cents a bushel. I had hit the big time! To pick from the trees, you were issued a ladder which was pointed on the upper end. This was so you could more easily place the ladder into a branch of the tree without damaging apples. Also, you were issued a metal bucket with a canvas bottom. Straps attached the bucket in front of you about waist high. As you filled the bucket, you carefully released the apples into a wooden bushel box. I wasn't as fast as the hired hands from Nova Scotia, but I made enough money to make me feel like I was getting up in the world. I can still remember the foreman telling me to "handle them like eggs, only faster." As I picked apples, I became aware of the farm machinery used in the orchard.

This farm had a couple of trucks to haul the apples to either the cider mill or to the market. One of the customers was Table Talk Pies in Worcester, Massachusetts. They also had a forklift Ford tractor, an International W4 tractor, and a bulldozer. I put in a request to the farm manager to move me from picking apples to driving the farm machinery. I was 15 years old and felt capable of driving anything. Heck, I drove that miniature Model T Ford at Whalom Park when I was only seven years old. I could handle this. Before long, my request was granted, and I was assigned to work with the foreman's son who was about my age. The main vehicle that we would be using was the International W4 tractor. It was used to haul bushel boxes to various strategic places in the orchard and haul boxes filled with apples to a central point where they would be hand loaded onto a pallet and forklifted on to a truck.

I was now earning $1.15 an hour and one season I earned $70 in one week! That was a lot of money back in 1959. It was a great accomplishment, and I still remember what it felt like to work hard and reap the rewards. I think that time in my life formed my work ethic for the rest of my life.

That International W4 tractor was basically the first full size vehicle that I drove.

The W4 was old at the time, but it was a bullet proof machine. We used it to load boxes of apples between rows of trees by putting it in a low gear, putting the engine at idle, releasing the clutch, stepping off, and letting the tractor move slowly all by itself as we loaded the trailer.

International W4 tractor like the one I learned to drive at the age of 15. These tractors were easy to work on and built to last.

It was a dangerous tractor because it had big fenders. If it ever started to roll over, the only exit option was to the rear and on to the tongue of the trailer. The exhaust exited in a straight pipe up through the cowling. On occasion, we would have a little fun by stomping an apple into the end of the pipe and then starting the engine. The exhaust pressure would quickly build up and blow the apple about a hundred feet into the air! The sweet smell like baked apple pie was in the air all around us. Nice memory.

There were other thrills with this machine that I still remember—like doing wheelies by popping the clutch, or unexpectedly skidding backward down a slippery steep hill without tipping over or jackknifing the trailer. I'm glad my parents didn't know about all these incidents. It would have been the end of my farming career.

Small farm bulldozer like the one we used for pushing pruning brush into big piles for burning.

CHAPTER 2

As I spent more time working in the apple orchard, I became familiar with some of the other farm machinery and got to drive them. The bulldozer, with a large wooden rake attached to the front, was used to push brush from the winter pruning to clearings within the orchard. The brush piles were then burned using gasoline and old tires to start and feed the fire. One time, when I was driving the bulldozer on a hill, it started to slide sideways on the wet grass. Some quick evasive action was required to keep the machine from rolling over. Farms and farm machinery are dangerous, and you could easily get gravely injured if you did not keep your wits about you. I was lucky.

The flatbed truck was used to transport apples to market, whether to a pie company in Worcester, or the cider mill in Stowe. Because I wasn't sixteen yet and didn't have my license, I only got to drive the truck within the orchard. Eventually when I got my license, I did drive loads of apples to Zander's Cider Mill. During a delivery, we weighed the truck on the scale when we arrived and then unloaded the apples. During the unloading process we could hear the workers yelling that there was a rat about to be pressed with the apples! How disgusting! Apparently, the press operation continued like nothing happened because we heard no more yelling. As we were weighing our unloaded truck to leave, old man Zander came out with a freshly pressed jug of cider and said, "here boys, take this with you." Knowing what happened to the rat, we never drank cider from that jug, and it was a long time before I ever drank apple cider again.

Flatbed farm truck for hauling apples to market and to the cider mill.

The Deuce Coupe that Stole My Heart

In my junior year of high school I was about to turn 16. Since my birthday was at the end of the year, I was one of the youngest students in my class of 1962. I took a driver's education class in school to get my license. At the time, my dad still had a 1950 Pontiac which he had bought new. My sister had her license, so she would take me out to practice driving. The Pontiac had a big six-cylinder engine and a three-speed manual transmission with the shifter lever on the column ('three on a tree' as they used to say). I had no problem driving a stick shift since I already had a couple years of practice on the farm. I do remember successfully turning around on a steep hill. It was a piece of cake after driving farm machinery.

Once you learn to drive a stick shift it is like riding a bicycle. You never forget. Years later, the transition to automatic transmissions slowly became popular and I'm sure there are many people today who have never driven a vehicle with a manual transmission. They don't know what they are missing! I think it is fun to "go through the gears."

Eventually, my dad traded in his 1950 Pontiac and bought a new Dodge Seneca from a local dealer. The old Pontiac sat in the dealer's lot for a few weeks. Now that I had my driver's license I was looking to buy my first car. Then it dawned on me, why not buy my dad's old car that was sitting on the dealer's back lot? I knew the history of the car and that it had been well taken care of, so I approached the dealer and he sold it to me for $50. I was the proud owner of my first car! I practiced driving on the back roads of our town to build up my confidence. There were no rules in those days - like being on a probation period, no driving at night, or no other kids in the car. And no seatbelts. Back then, when you got your license as a new driver, you just hit the road. No wonder insurance was so high for kids under the age of 25.

1950 Pontiac like my first car. These came with either a straight six or straight eight cylinder engine.

I started to drive myself to school every day, and to the apple orchard for my job in the afternoon. It was good to experience the independence of having your own vehicle and the freedom that came with it. It didn't take long before I began to hot rod the Pontiac. It started with nosing and decking the hood and trunk lid. This consisted of removing the chrome trim and filling the holes by either welding or using Bondo plastic filler. Since this was a four-door sedan, I wanted to make it look like a two-door car so I removed the rear door handles and filled those holes as well. A friend from high school worked at a garage in the neighboring town of Lancaster, so I paid him a visit one day and he applied oxyacetylene torch heat to the front coil springs to lower the front end. After a paint job in the driveway with a borrowed spray gun and compressor, the car was looking pretty cool in my estimation.

I got the brilliant idea to replace the original transmission with a floor shift type from a LaSalle automobile. LaSalle (1927 to 1940) was a brand of car made by the Cadillac division of General Motors. I found a donor car in a junk yard near me and transplanted the transmission into the Pontiac. Looking back, I only used a bumper jack to lift the car up to replace the transmission. Stupid kid! Now I am smarter and,

LaSalle car (1927-1940) that donated a transmission with floor shifter to my Pontiac.

Richard Stoebel

while working under a car, I use jack stands and substantial wood bracing under the wheels. It is amazing the dumb things you do as a kid and live to talk about it. God must have been looking over my shoulder.

I eventually put a glass packed muffler in the exhaust system to get that throaty sound. Since we had to have our cars inspected once a year in Massachusetts, I drilled a hole in the tailpipe, stuffed steel wool in the pipe and inserted a long bolt through the drilled holes to keep the wool in place. This temporarily quieted the exhaust. After inspection, the bolt was removed, and with a few bursts of power the steel wool was blown out.

My hot rod was pretty nice but lacked the power to do burnouts. I discovered that reverse was geared so low, that I could leave a 100-foot-long strip of rubber doing a burnout in reverse! I remember doing this as I was parking the car on a side street at the high school. I thought I was cool.

Another guy in town had a car for sale that I really admired. It was a 1950 Oldsmobile 88 with a big Rocket V8 engine. It had the reputation of being able to do burnouts in first and second gear. The evidence of that could be seen all over our town and the neighboring towns. It was a pretty car, nosed and decked with a nice paint job. I wanted that car in the worst way, but my parents would not let me buy it. It was a big disappointment, but they knew it was a powerful and dangerous car to drive. I probably would have killed myself with that car. It was just not meant to be.

The Deuce Coupe that Stole My Heart

1950 Oldsmobile Rocket 88. The one that my parents wouldn't let me buy. The engine only put out 135 HP, but produced lots of torque.

CHAPTER 3

I hand-painted cool looking flames on the Pontiac front fenders—just to the rear of the wheels—like ones I had seen on hot rods in car magazines, I have always liked the look of flames on a hot rod.

One day, my sister borrowed the car to pick up my mom. As people were getting out of work, some guy yelled over to my sister and said, "Hey, lady, your wheels are on fire!" Eventually, I painted over the flames to spare any more embarrassment. Maybe it wasn't such a good idea afterall. I knew that somewhere in my future I would have another hot rod with professionally applied flames on it. After high school graduation in the spring of 1962, I was accepted into the aircraft maintenance program (AM64) at Wentworth Institute in Boston. I drove my Pontiac there and parked it in front of the dormitory. After a few months at school, I decided to sell the car to some friends back in my hometown. I needed the money for school and could not

1955 Chevrolet. The first of the tri-five series 1955-1957.

afford to continue paying insurance on the car. Faced with not having a car for a couple of years, I met up with some classmates that lived near my hometown. One of the guys, Frank Putnam, had a 1955 Chevy with a 283 cubic inch V8 in it. He had done a little work on the exhaust system, and it sounded nice. We used this car to get home during school breaks. We both liked cars and mechanical things in general, so we became lifelong friends.

After graduation from Wentworth, I got a job working in the apple orchard for the summer before starting my new full-time job as a mechanic at Pratt & Whitney Aircraft Engines in East Hartford, Connecticut. I needed a car to get around, so I found a rear engine 1960 Chevy Corvair for sale

The Deuce Coupe that Stole My Heart

1960 Corvair with air cooled rear engine. The Corvair was manufactured by Chevrolet from 1960 to 1969.

at a used car lot in the neighboring town of Bolton.

I also found out that the previous owner was a pretty girl who lived not far away. We started dating a few times.

On one of the dates, we decided to go "parking" at the apple orchard where I had worked. One night we were going into the orchard with the headlights on and we were spotted by a neighbor who knew me. It wasn't long after we were "parked" that we were paid a visit by the neighbor and a friend of his. They cunningly greeted us and then proceeded to open the trunk lid and remove a bunch of ignition wires from the engine! I guess it was their idea of fun. They laughed and said, "Enjoy the rest of your evening" and disappeared into the dark of night. We were left there with no option but to try to get all the wires back in place or be stranded for the night. I got out of the car, opened the rear hood and, with the dim light of the compartment, painstakingly put everything back together. It took a while, but when I started the engine it fired right up. I got lucky with the car but not with the girl that night! During one of my trips to Connecticut for my job at Pratt, the Corvair started to lose power and then finally quit leaving me stuck at the side of the road. I noticed a gas station a way back, so I hopped the divided highway fence and thumbed a ride back to the station. They had a tow truck, so it wasn't long before the Corvair was retrieved. The problem turned out to be the fuel pump. The push rod had worn to a point where the pump could not be fully actuated. The station could not find a new or used one in short order, so they opted to weld a little material on to the end of the rod. It worked well enough to get me back to East Hartford. I found a local repair station near my apartment that could replace the fuel pump, but I was out of money because of the highway tow job and quick repair. (This was back in the day before credit cards.) Luckily, the repair shop extended credit until my next payday and trusted me to return with the payment. After a week, I returned to the repair shop and paid in full. I was grateful that the owner of the shop trusted me to clear my debt with him. I gave him business for years after that and thanked him every chance I got.

Sometime later, I was back in Massachusetts visiting my folks. I was headed on an errand to the neighboring town of Bolton. On my way there, something failed in the drive train of the Corvair. The engine was still running but could not deliver the power to the rear wheels. I shifted into neutral and, since I was headed down a long steep hill, I glided all the way to the bottom, through the intersection in the center of town and into the parking lot where I had bought the car! They diagnosed the problem as a broken shaft, so I decided to sell the car back to them, which they agreed to. It was time to get another, more reliable car.

In 1965 (actually 1964-½) Ford had just come out with the Mustang. Ironically, my sister and I both decided to buy new Mustangs because they were very popular at the time. The one I chose was a yellow coupe with a 289 cubic inch V8 engine and a four-speed transmission. The shift lever was on the floor which was what I liked. I could leave rubber with this car in first and second gear because the engine was powerful and the car so light. This would be my hot rod for the near future.

I was now working at Pratt & Whitney as a mechanic in the experimental assembly and test department. The job paid well, but it was the first time I had ever punched a time clock and I didn't like it. Before too long, I got a job as an engineering aide in the mechanical components group. I traded the hourly job for a white-collar salary position. This was more to my liking. It didn't take me long to realize that if I went back to school to get my bachelor's degree in engineering, I could double my salary. I applied to three schools, Embry Riddle in Florida, Parks Institute in Chicago, and Northrop Institute in California. I got my earliest reply from Northrop Institute, and they accepted most of my credits from Wentworth.

1965 Mustang. My first new car. Introduced as a 1964-½ model, the Mustang sold one million copies in its first two years. It is still in production as of this writing.

With the backing of my folks, I was encouraged to continue with my education. They even took over the payments of my Mustang while I was gone. I had great parents and would forever be grateful to them for their help so I could go back to school. It was off to California for me.

CHAPTER 4

Northrop Institute was founded to train aviation mechanics to work in the airplane industry. After a while, they began offering Bachelor of Science degrees. I enrolled in the Aircraft Maintenance program, BSAME. The school was in Inglewood, not too far from Los Angeles International Airport.

I lived near the school but felt I needed transportation to get around, work a job in my spare time, and visit my relatives in Palos Verdes Estates just south of LA. My first motorcycle was a Honda 50cc. It was just barely adequate to get me around, so I sold it and bought a recovered Honda 305 Scrambler. It had been repossessed by an insurance company after being stolen and abandoned. I restored the motorcycle into good working order. That was my go-to transportation for most of my stay in the Golden State. At some point in time, I was loaned a 650cc Triumph Bonneville motorcycle by an acquaintance who, of all things, was in trouble with the law. He needed to leave the state for a while. The bike was fast, and I swear I would have gotten into trouble with it sooner or later if it was mine. I was glad when the "outlaw" finally came back to reclaim it!

Top: Honda 305 Scrambler motorcycle. My main transportation while going to college in California. Used on and off road.

Bottom: Triumph 650 Bonneville. A powerful street motorcycle that I had for a brief time in California

One of my roommates had a black 1957 Chevy convertible with a three-speed shifter on the floor. We traded motorcycle for car and vice-versa as the need arose. My roommate wanted

The Deuce Coupe that Stole My Heart

to drive to Maine from California for a Christmas visit with his family. Before he took off, he drove up and down the alleys where rubbish was put out for collection and he found four pretty good tires. He had them mounted on the Chevy and drove the entire round trip to Maine and back without incident. Upon his return, he got a flat tire right in the garage of our apartment complex! He was a lucky guy.

The first Christmas in California, I flew back to Connecticut. The following Christmas, I hooked up with three other students to drive back to New England. One of the guys had a mid-60s Ford Thunderbird and we all took turns driving it nonstop from coast to coast. It took us 56 hours, stopping only for food, gas, and bathroom breaks. One memorable part of the trip was traveling through New Mexico at 100 miles per hour and blowing a right rear tire. Swerving side to side from road to desert, we finally came to a stop without flipping the car. One lug nut was frozen in place, so we had to cold chisel it off. Other cars were coming

1957 Chevrolet convertible like the one my roommate had in California. I traded my motorcycle for this car on accasion.

by us at 100 mph, and it would shake our car while it was up on a bumper jack. It was very unnerving.

1960 Ford Thunderbird. We drove this car from California to New England and back for Christmas break.

When I graduated from Northrop, I got a job back at Pratt & Whitney in Connecticut in an experimental engineering department. In my new engineering job in the JT9D experimental group we were developing the engine for the Boeing 747.

I retrieved my Mustang from my parents and resumed the payments. At this time, I also took a lien on the Mustang and bought a 1946 Piper J3 Cub airplane, but that is a story for another time.

Soon I got the itch to own a Corvette. I impulsively bought a 1960 powder blue convertible with white side panels and sold my 1965 Mustang. The Corvette had an automatic transmission, so I had a local hot rod shop switch it over to a three-speed standard shift transmission. At this point in my life, I owned an airplane and a Corvette. Life was good.

1960 Corvette. I removed the automatic transmission and replaced it with a three-speed manual shifter.

The Corvette lost some of its appeal when I got married in 1969 and we bought our first house in 1970. I had been assigned to engineering duty in Middletown, Connecticut and it was about a 40-mile commute. My wife, Brenda, had a 1968 Firebird and it did not make sense to have two muscle cars along with a new house and a baby on the way. So, the Corvette was sold off and I bought a used Volkswagen Beetle to travel to work. There goes bachelorhood, hello married life! I had that Beetle for a couple of years, but the body started to rust out in the rocker panels and floorboards. It was time for a new car.

One day I stopped at the Ford dealer in the neighboring town of Glastonbury on my way home from work. They had a new 1972 Ford Pinto hatchback in the showroom that I

Richard Stoebel

1968 Pontiac Firebird. My wife's first car which she bought brand new. The 8-track tape entertainment system was stolen out of this car—twice.

Volkswagen Beetle. A great commuter car for traveling to work from Coventry, Connecticut to Middletown.

The Deuce Coupe that Stole My Heart

really liked. It had an upgraded engine, four speed shift lever on the floor, nice wheels, and a few optional items like a sunroof. I called my wife, and she gave me the thumbs up to purchase it. The Pinto got a lot of use over the coming 12 years and 120,000 miles.

Not too long after I bought it, I was at lunch one day with a fellow engineer. As we were leaving the burger joint, the parking lot was full of lunchtime customers. There was a dirt lot next door where truckers would pull in for lunch, so I decided to just drive through the mud puddle at the edge of the paved parking lot and go out the truck exit. As I went through the brown, muddy puddle I was surprised that it was deeper than I thought—about a foot and a half deep to be exact! How embarrassing to exit the puddle with steam coming up from the quenched hot exhaust and possible damage to the car. I did a walk around and everything looked okay, but it was a little later that I realized the clutch throw out bearing had been immersed in crud and made the bearing noisy. Every time I changed gears from that point on, and for the rest of the life of the car, I was reminded of how dumb it was to drive through that water.

We used that car to travel to Florida with our two-year-old daughter. I was assigned to run an engine program in West Palm Beach. We had the option of flying or driving. We decided to drive down with the Pinto. Little did we know there was going to be a safety recall on the car. If the car was hit in the rear hard enough, the impact could drive the gas tank into the rear end resulting in gas leakage and the

1972 Ford Pinto Hatchback. Purchased new and sold after 10 years and 120,000 miles.

possibility of fire. Our daughter slept in the back of the vehicle among our luggage for this Florida trip. We were lucky that nothing ever happened to us.

Years later, I was driving through the parking lot at work with the Pinto when the right front inner fender well broke off and I ran over it. As I looked at the part in my rear-view mirror, I knew it was time to get rid of the car and move on to something newer. I put the Pinto up for sale on our bulletin board at work and sold it right out of the parking lot.

CHAPTER 5

The Ford Model T was built from 1908 to 1927 with over 15 million cars produced. The "Tin Lizzy" was a low-cost car that the masses of people could afford. Because the cars were so cheap, my dad told me of a funny little quip that people used to say about them. "A little spark, a little coil, a little spring, a little oil, a piece of tin and a two-inch board, put them together and you've got a Ford." That's probably why he never owned one. One the first cars he owned was an Overland.

Even the more expensive cars back in the early 1900s had growing pain mechanical troubles. One day, the Overland engine was not running well, so my dad took it to a repair shop. The mechanic assessed the problem, told my dad to park it in the sun, open the hood and just let it sit there for a few hours. When my dad came back to pick up the car, the engine started and it ran smoothly again. It must have just been moisture in the ignition system. No charge from the mechanic. My dad drove that Overland from Clinton,

1926 Overland (Willys). My dad drove this car 450 miles to Niagara Falls. Probably more durable than a Ford, but still with common mechanical problems.

Massachusetts to Niagara Falls for a family vacation one time. That was a 450-mile trip one way over unimproved roads. Quite an adventure all those years ago.

Early spark plug parts disassembled for cleaning. Plugs would foul easily because of leaded fuel and poor combustion.

The Deuce Coupe that Stole My Heart

I have a small spark plug collection. Because some of the older plugs would often get fouled with carbon, they could be disassembled for cleaning and I have a few of these. In today's technology, spark plugs don't have to be cleaned and they don't have to be changed for 100,000 miles. We've come a long way baby!

In my hometown in central Massachusetts, there was a window washer who serviced all the businesses in downtown Clinton. He had a Ford Model A pickup truck that he used to transport all his ladders and equipment. I always admired that truck. One day when I was shopping downtown and doing some errands, I noticed a crowd gathered around on the sidewalk. As I approached the gathering, I could see the window washer sprawled out on his back on the pavement. He had fallen off his ladder from two or three stories up. I'm not sure what his injuries consisted of, but after that incident I never saw the window washer or his truck in the downtown area again. I've often wondered what happened to that old truck that I admired so much.

I was drawn to old Ford cars and trucks for some reason. Chevrolet cars did not interest me unless we were talking about the tri-five series (1955 through 1957). I admired other cars such as Cord, Studebaker, and pickup trucks in general, but I always gravitated to 1932, 1933, 1934, 1937, and 1940 Fords. It didn't matter if they were coupes, roadsters, cabriolets, phaetons, or pickup trucks. Two-door sedans were nice too, but four-door cars in general didn't appeal to me at all. Coupes were usually produced in three-window and five-window configurations. A three-window

Ford Model A pickup. Built from 1928 to 1931. A classic truck design.

coupe had a rear window and a side window in each door. The windshield was not counted. Conversely, a five-window coupe consisted of a rear window, a side window in each door and a quarter side window behind each door.

Roadsters and cabriolets were similar in that they had a soft top that could fold down. A roadster had side curtains that could be put in place during inclement weather. The cabriolet had roll up windows in the doors. Coupes and roadsters came with either a trunk lid or a rumble seat. The last year for rumble seats in the Ford product line was 1939 because of safety reasons. Cars were traveling faster and faster with bigger engines and improved roads. If you got hit in the rear, occupants in the rumble seat could be severely injured. A sudden stop from a front-end collision was even worse. Rumble seat occupants could be propelled forward and sometimes decapitated! There were no seatbelts back then. Phaetons were like an elongated roadster with seating for four people. They came in either two-door or four-door

The Deuce Coupe that Stole My Heart

1932 Ford three-window coupe. One model of the iconic deuce coupe series.

1932 Ford five-window coupe like the one I modified into a deuce coupe hot rod.

versions. The four-door phaeton was the only four-door 1930s car that appealed to me.

Spare tires on many of these cars were mounted on the back, almost like continental kits that became popular years later. Spare tires could also be mounted in front fender wells, either single (usually on the driver's side) or dual sides. Some cars also had exterior trunks added to the back for extra storage.

The 1932 Ford car seems to stand out. It was the first year Ford introduced a V8 engine. The flathead V8 put out a whopping 65 horsepower. That year also still had a four-cylinder version, the Model B, which put out 50 horsepower. The 1932 body style was a one-year unique design that was roomier than its Model A predecessors. Hot rod and racing enthusiasts gravitated to this car like no other. Speed equipment came on the market to feed the demand for faster and faster cars. The "little deuce coupe" was featured in movies like *American Graffiti*. Of the 275,000 Ford

1932 Ford Cabriolet. With roll-up windows, this model was more of an all-weather car

1932 Ford Roadster. Cheaper than a Cabriolet, it used side curtains for protection during inclement weather.

Early Ford rumble seat. Fun to ride in, but dangerous during an accident. Rumble seats were phased out in 1939.

Early Ford Phaeton two-door sedan. A nice family car with seating for four people. Not for the faint of heart in the cold of winter.

Early Ford Phaeton four-door sedan. A four-passenger version of an open car similar to a Roadster.

Side mounted spare tire. Classic fender well mounting that could be single or dual.

passenger cars produced in 1932, 185,000 were equipped with the V8 engine. And these cars were sold during the Great Depression following the stock market crash of 1929. Helping to popularize the 1932 Ford, Clyde Barrow, of Bonnie and Clyde fame, even wrote a letter to Henry Ford thanking him for his fine and fast V8 powered car!

Of the cars that followed the 1932 Ford, the 1933 and 1934 models incorporated some design changes like the rear sloping grille and grille shell. The only distinction between the two Model years that is readily discernible is the 1933 had slightly concave grille "teeth" and the 1934 had straight grille "teeth." The Ford cars of these years no longer offered a four-cylinder engine. They all had the new V8 engine. There were other minor changes between the 1933 and 1934 models, but the grille is the most prominent.

The 1937 cars were always considered the ugly ducklings of the late 1930s Fords but were popular for round track racing of that era. Many of these cars were raced, wrecked, and scrapped during the post-World War II years. 1937 was the first year that Ford embedded the headlights into the front fenders instead of mounting them on the fenders or on a light bar between the fenders. This was also the first year that Ford incorporated a full metal roof. Chevy had beat them to market in prior years, but Ford finally caught up with metal stamping machines that could produce these larger panels. Prior to this year, Ford was still using the old wood and fabric insert roof design that worked for many years. Ford also produced a smaller, entry level version of the now

Richard Stoebel

Top: 1933 Ford grille with concave shape. An attempt at streamline styling.

Bottom: 1934 Ford grille with a straight shape. A subtle change from the 1933 version.

85 horsepower flathead V8 engine. They called it the baby V8 that produced 60 horsepower. This smaller engine would be phased out in 1940.

1937 Ford front view. Note headlights in fenders and filled roof. Ford finally abandoned the wood and fabric tops used in earlier years.

Richard Stoebel

"A little spring,
a little oil.
A little spark,
a little coil.
A piece of tin
and a 2 inch board.
Put them together
and you've got a *Ford*."

—*Henry Stoebel* —

CHAPTER 6

As a young family man with a wife, new baby, new house, and all the responsibilities that go along with it, I still had the desire to build a hot rod. The iconic 1932 Ford was one of my favorite cars. If I was going to build one, I needed to start collecting parts. There was an Old Ford Store in downtown Manchester, Connecticut. I visited there often, and, on one occasion, I spotted a 1932 Ford frame. These frames were unique because it was the only year that Ford used the frame as part of the body styling. The sculpted frame with a beauty line along its length was visible between the body and the running boards. This frame would be the basis for my project car.

I needed a drive train for this project. I came across a running V6 Buick engine and automatic transmission that would be perfect. I bought the engine and transmission and stuffed it away in the corner of our garage. Next I needed a front axle and rear end to get the chassis off the ground and on wheels (considered a rolling chassis). With the pressures of work, business travel and another baby on the way, it just did not make sense to try to continue with this car project. And so, I sold off the 1932 Ford frame and Buick engine to make room for the next phase of my life—finding a new house for my family.

We lived in Coventry, Connecticut at the time but all our shopping and activities took place in Manchester. It just made sense to move to Manchester if the opportunity arose and it would be a shorter commute to work. One weekend as we were driving around we spotted a Tudor style colonial house with a sign out front that said, "foreclosure auction." The house, I estimated, was about 75% complete and the builder had declared bankruptcy. As (bad) luck would have it, we did not act fast enough to purchase the house at auction, but we did strike up a deal with the new broker to pay him a few thousand dollars over what he paid for the house. He wouldn't have to lift a finger to make a sizable profit. He agreed to the deal.

Over the next six months, I worked on the new house. We eventually sold off our other house in Coventry. This would be the home and neighborhood we would live in and raise our kids in for the next 27 years.

Of course, it didn't take long before I got the itch to have an old Ford. I found an original 1932 Ford five window coupe down in Norwich, Connecticut. It was a Model B with the four-cylinder engine. I think I bought this car for around $5000, and the seller drove it to our house. The car had a rumble seat and side mounted spare tires. Occasionally, my wife and I would jump into the car, throw our two children into the rumble seat and drive it around the neighborhood just for fun. It probably wasn't the smartest thing to do since the car was not registered and we had no liability insurance on it. We drove it, nevertheless. We were young and foolish.

My first 1932 Ford coupe, unrestored. This was a five-window, rumble seat Model B with a four-cylinder engine.

Our young kids were fooling around in the garage one day and climbed up into the rumble seat. Our son decided to jump out of the seat and over the rear fender. He tripped and landed on his head on the cement garage floor. I still cringe at the sound of him hitting the floor. We scooped him up and took him to the emergency room. After some time in the hospital, it was determined that he had a concussion but would recover without any lasting effects. We were lucky that the accident was not more serious. . This reminds me of an old saying that my dad used to tell me. "It's a good thing you hit your head, otherwise you might have gotten hurt." Thanks dad, for that wise advice.

The coupe was stored in our walkout basement for the winter months. We had a double door opening at ground level that was just wide enough to push the coupe through. It was probably not the wisest place to keep an old vehicle with gasoline in it next to a gas furnace, but I was vigilant to frequently check the car for leaks. We really needed a house with a bigger garage, but this was not the time in our lives to be thinking about that. We had the coupe for a couple of years. It became evident once again that pressures from work, family and life were too busy to also own and maintain an old car. And so, we put the coupe up for sale. A couple from the neighboring town of South Windsor bought it. We made a small profit on the sale of the car. I was sad to see it go, but there would be another one in my future, I was fairly sure of that.

Some years passed during which we owned a couple of boats. It was nice to be able to take the family out on the water and enjoy cruising around, water skiing and swimming on a sizzling summer day. When my son was about 12 years old, we took our 18-foot Bayliner Cuddy Cabin down the Connecticut River from Hartford to Old Saybrook. It was a 44-mile trip and it took all day. We both had secured our safe boating license in preparation for this trip. At one point, as

The Deuce Coupe that Stole My Heart

we tried to enter Long Island Sound, the traffic and rough water was too much for our small boat. We took a wave over the bow, over the windshield and canvas, and into the back of the boat. It was time to turn around and head back to avoid getting swamped. We would need a bigger boat or ideal conditions to get out on to the Sound. My son drove the boat all the way back to Hartford. I was pretty proud of him. They say that the two best times in a boat owner's life is when you purchase a boat and when you sell it. So we put the boat and trailer up for sale. I had a Ford Thunderbird at the time, and this is what I used to haul the boat around. It was not the best vehicle for this task, but I nursed it up hills and on slippery boat ramps. We sold the boat and eventually sold the Thunderbird. It was time for a new chapter in our life.

1985 Ford Thunderbird. A family car that I occasionally towed my boat with. A style popularized by Bill Elliot, the Winston Cup Series race car driver.

CHAPTER 7

A friend, Larry Krizan, had built a beautiful 1936 Ford cabriolet. It had a strong Chevy 350 cubic inch engine and a four-speed manual transmission. He let me drive it one time and as we were going down the on ramp to the highway he said "Don't baby it. Put your foot into it!" I punched the throttle and that car took off! It got my hot rod juices flowing, so I started to look around for a project car.

I was working at Pratt & Whitney and the job was really stressful. My doctor recommended that I start a hobby to get my mind off work. So, the time was now right to start another car project.

I found out about a 1937 Ford Tudor sedan that was for sale and stored in a barn in a neighboring town. I went over to check it out. When the barn door opened, I immediately fell in love with the car. It was a slantback sedan body which to me was more desirable than the hump-back trunk version.

It had no engine or transmission but was on a rolling chassis. The interior was devoid of a front seat and steering column but all the hard-to-find door handles, window cranks, and instrument panel were intact. The price was $450 which I thought was a good deal. I paid for the car and hired a guy with a flatbed truck to take it to my home.

When the car was delivered, my wife took one look at it and said, "you paid good money for that?" She obviously wasn't happy about the purchase, but I could see the potential in this old car. I was going to do some restoration work on the body and put a modern drive train in it. The first task was to remove the gas tank which still had residual fuel in it. The bolts holding it in place were frozen, so I carefully applied heat to the fasteners with a torch. I did this out in the driveway just in case the thing blew up. I removed the fenders which were in fairly good shape except for a couple of dents. I also sand blasted the body in the driveway to clean up and reveal any rusted panels. After that was finished, I moved the car into the garage to start body work. There was some rot in the floor pan near the trunk and some rust in the rocker and quarter panels that needed attention.

I built a wooden gantry and used a come-along to lift the body off the frame and to install the engine and transmission. It did not take long to fix the problem areas and get the body into primer. All the welding was done with an oxy acetylene torch. I taught myself the techniques of hammer welding and shrinking the metal by quenching. Welding is an art form that I initially learned in aviation mechanics school. It really came in handy for this project.

The Deuce Coupe that Stole My Heart

Gantry to lift engine & trans into the '37 Ford. A simple way to get the job done if you do not have an overhead lift.

Now I needed a drive train for the car. I wanted to stay with a Ford engine instead of the Chevy engines that most hot rod folks used. I found a 1967 Ford station wagon for sale with a 289 cubic inch engine and automatic transmission for a few hundred bucks. I drove the car over to Roger Billard's farm in Amston, Connecticut where we removed the drive train. The plan was to transplant the engine, transmission, shortened driveshaft, and rear end into the 1937 Ford. I also stripped the station wagon of instruments and other components that I might be able to use. The shell of the station wagon went to the junk yard and my friend delivered the drive train to my house. The agreed price for his help was my Marlin lever action .22 rifle which he always admired. I loved that gun. It was very accurate and in beautiful shape. I regret letting that gun go to this day. I tried to buy it back from Roger many times over the years and the answer was always "I don't think so."

Now the hard work began to clean up the engine, transmission and rear end, and install it in the chassis. It required hand fabricated engine mounts and modification of the frame. I did not split the front wishbone radius rods as some people do, but was able to lower the rear attachment point with spacers to provide clearance for the transmission mount. The rear end was installed, and driveshaft shortened to fit. The gas tank was cleaned and sealed and all fuel and brake plumbing was completed.

There were no wiring kits available for this car back then, so I drew up a complete wiring diagram and started the installation. The wire came from work. A test stand fuel pump room was being rebuilt at Pratt & Whitney and the contents of the room were being stripped. On a nightly basis, as I walked through the area during second and third shift engineering coverage, I pulled wire of different colors and gauges out of the 50-gallon barrels and took it home. This was the source of all the wire that went into the '37. It was a low buck project.

After the body work and mechanicals were completed, it was time for some paint. I purchased a few quarts of brown acrylic lacquer and some thinner and on a calm day went to work in the driveway. I sprayed three or four coats on and then wet sanded everything. It turned out pretty good for a

1937 Ford sedan in our driveway during restoration. I can still hear my wife saying, "You paid good money for this?"

driveway paint job. Some cream-colored double pin striping was applied along the upper beauty line of the car and the exterior was complete. Not bad for an amateur. The '37 came without a steering column or steering box. My friend Larry said, "I think I can dig one up for you," and he quite literally dug one up with his backhoe! He had buried an unused column in his back yard after completing his project car. Some cleaning, primer and paint and the column was ready to be installed. The steering box still had good grease in it! A banjo steering wheel from another friend completed the steering hookup. I found a front seat in the woods in Union,

Richard Stoebel

Connecticut and purchased an upholstery kit from an old car supply business.

I tried to install a headliner kit but was having trouble getting the wrinkles out, so I contacted a guy by the name of Bob Juliano who ran a hot rod and upholstery shop over in Vernon, Connecticut. He came to our house with some equipment, a heat gun and a couple of other guys. They had that headliner installed in under an hour. The cost? No charge. He did it as a favor. And, so, I paid him to install the carpeting. Because of his help, I did business with Bob many times over the years. He was the quintessential hot-rodder and a good friend.

After the car was completed, I drove it to my parent's house in central Massachusetts, kind of like a shakedown cruise. I gave my mom and dad a ride in it, and they were pleased with my handiwork. The car made it all the way without any problems on that 200-mile round trip! I must have done something right during the build. On another occasion my wife, Brenda, took the car for an errand with her sister Karen in the passenger seat. When they returned, she remarked "did you know the '37 can leave rubber if you really put your foot into it?" I've always contended that her right foot was bigger than her left, and she just proved me right again!

The Deuce Coupe that Stole My Heart

Larry Krizan's 1936 Ford Cabriolet and my 1937 Ford Tudor sedan. Getting ready to drive to a nearby car show.

CHAPTER 8

We owned and maintained the 1937 Ford for a few years but then it was time to move on. I think I actually enjoyed building these cars as much as I did driving them, maybe more. It is a challenge to be sure, and a lot of work. After spending an intense year building the car, I swore that I would never build another one.

To sell the '37, I advertised in *Hemmings Motor News* and finally got a buyer to come up from New Jersey to take a look. After a test drive and a thorough inspection we agreed upon a price of $5,500 cash. I built the car for about $5000 in parts and miscellaneous costs, and a gun. The labor was free. I certainly enjoyed the car. The buyer drove the car back to New Jersey and I never heard from him again. I can only hope that somebody is still taking good care of it. I regret that I let a spare '37 grille shell go with the car. They are hard to find and expensive. It would have looked nice hanging on my garage wall.

Richard Stoebel

Years passed without having a hot rod in the garage. We were busy with work, house, children's activities, and life. There were always projects to do around the house and we saved a lot of money by doing most of them ourselves.

It was inevitable that the hot rod bug would bite me again. I was still looking for a 1932 Ford but had interest in other years as well. I appreciated all makes and years of these special interest cars and trucks, but I was just more interested in certain ones. There is a lot of information online. Over the years I have bought two hot rods and five or six family cars online. This time I was perusing the cars on www.hotrodhotline.com. I spotted a 1930 Ford roadster in California. It was a rumble seat model with a 300 horsepower 327 cubic inch Chevy engine built by a race car engine guy and a 1968 Jaguar independent suspension rear end. The roadster was painted Porsche Indian Red acrylic enamel and had wire wheels. The grille and grille shell were original '32 Ford with a custom louvered hood to match. It was a California car and because of the dry desert climate, it had no rust and needed no patch panels.

I received a package from the owner, Richard Wickert, with photos and a build sheet describing details of the car. The builder, Jim Garcia, had completed the car and brought it to the LA Roadster show in Pomona. Jim, as I was to find out, had built a number of cars over the years for a number of clients. He was very good at fabrication and was known for building bullet proof cars. Richard bought the roadster at that show. He made a few changes to the car over time. He removed the high performance camshaft and replaced it with a milder one. He also made some changes to the front end installing a chrome dropped tube axle. To my knowledge, those were the majority of changes made to the original hot rod.

Richard continued the legacy of taking the car to the LA Roadster show over the next 16 years. The show started back in 1956 and continues to this day. It is one of the largest pre-1936 roadster shows in the nation, held on Father's Day each year. The car was also featured in the June, 1990 swimsuit issue of *American Rodder* magazine, and later in the 1992 swimsuit calendar. With the rich history of this 1930 Ford roadster, I decided to strike up a deal to purchase the car. Arrangements were made to ship it to Connecticut via closed carrier. I still remember the moment the car was unloaded from the transport trailer. The car met every expectation I could have imagined. It was truly a nice looking and well-built hot rod.

I got temporary plates from the Motor Vehicle Department (MVD) and drove the car to Bob Juliano's shop for VIN verification and inspection. Since Bob was a car dealer, he was able to fulfill the inspection requirements of the MVD. Emission testing was not required on cars over 25 years old. I then was able to get license plates for the car. Connecticut required two license plates, one on the front and one on the back. Because the front plate did not lend itself well to the looks of the car, I just used the rear plate. I kept the front one somewhere in the car just in case I got stopped by the police or MVD inspectors.

Over the years I started to make changes to the roadster to personalize it to my liking. The handmade headers dumped into the exhaust pipe too low underneath the car which meant that occasionally I grounded out on that low point. And so, I bought a pair of aftermarket headers with a nice ceramic coating on them and fabricated new exhaust pipes. This modification gave me more ground clearance. Another addition that I made was to add a soft top. When driving the car at highway speeds, the wind hit the flat, chopped, windshield and whipped you on the back of the head enough to knock your hat off. I had to do something about that.

I ordered a set of irons and bows from one of the aftermarket antique parts suppliers. There were standard steel irons available and deluxe irons with polished stainless steel. I went with the deluxe set. Because the windshield was chopped, the soft top I was adding would have to be lowered, too. Modifications like this were done in the early days of racing at the Bonneville Salt Flats in Utah or El Mirage dry lake in California in order to lower the profile of the car and offer less wind resistance so it could go faster. After the irons and wood bows were modified, I took the car to an upholstery shop in Newington, Connecticut for the top material. When it was completed it was much more fun for me to drive the car in comfort. I still had the option of lowering the top on nice days, but I kept the top up most of the time.

The roadster had a rumble seat lid, but it was just an

The Deuce Coupe that Stole My Heart

empty trunk under it with no seat cushions or upholstery. I decided to finish the rumble seat so that I could give my grandkids a ride to experience what it was like back in the day. I ordered the seat springs and had a shop in Vernon, Connecticut upholster them in black tuck and roll to match the existing front seat. The roadster also came without rear bumpers, so I added them and installed step pads on the bumper and rear fender just like the original. Now I had a more complete car to enjoy with my family. I made changes to the roadster and had the satisfaction of doing it myself. Such is the joy of owning one of these old cars.

My 1930 Ford rumble seat roadster as purchased from California. No softtop installed at this time. The grandkids loved this car.

Roadster with soft top installed. Parts modified to match the chopped windshield.

CHAPTER 9

I enjoyed having the 1930 Ford roadster but storing it for the winter was a burden. It was taking up garage space that we needed for our family cars, and at least one of our personal cars would have to be out in the ice and snow in the driveway for the winter months. I did store it in our basement for a couple of winters, but I was now looking for an alternative storage space.

We had a neighbor across the street that had a two-car garage and only one car. I struck up a deal with her that if I could store the roadster in her garage for $50 a month, I would also snow blow and shovel her driveway and sidewalks for the duration of the winter. She agreed and the roadster was moved across the street, covered up and surrounded by mouse traps. (I always used mouse traps around the car because those little critters liked to climb into the engine compartment, build nests and chew on wiring. I caught a few of them during the first days of storage.) Little did I know

know that that winter was going to have the heaviest and most frequent snowfall of any recent years on record. I think our neighbor lady got the best part of the deal because at the end of the winter she took pity on me and waived the $50 monthly fee.

We were able to use this winter storage for a few years, so the roadster had a good place to stay nearby. It sure would have been nice to have a bigger garage, but that was not to be in the foreseeable future. That didn't stop me from dreaming of finally getting a 1932 Ford. I started to search online for a low-cost car but '32 Fords commanded a hefty price. I did finally find one out in Nebraska. It was a five-window coupe sitting on an aftermarket boxed frame. It had a nine-inch Ford rear end and a four-inch dropped front axle. It was on wheels, so it was considered a rolling chassis. There was no engine or transmission and no seat. It was pretty much bare bones.

This car was found abandoned in the Minnesota woods by a couple of game wardens. The frame was rusted badly, to the point that it could not be saved, and the lower ten inches of the body was in bad shape too. It was determined that the body could still be saved so it was pulled out of the woods and eventually sold to a chassis builder in Grand Island, Nebraska. The hot rod shop proceeded to do some body work to make it presentable and then set it on one of their new, boxed '32 Ford chassis. The car was painted in primer and put up for sale. After some negotiation, we agreed on a price of $16,000 plus another $1,000 for shipping to Connecticut. The car was

1932 Ford coupe as purchased from Nebraska. The beginning of what turned out to be an eight-year project

delivered a couple of weeks later by open carrier. There was no need to transport it in a more expensive closed trailer because it was just a shell of a vehicle. Now the planning and real work would begin.

The first thing I did was to remove the hood, doors, dash, and trunk lid, and sandblast the body out in the driveway. The blasting revealed a lot of issues that had to be corrected. The patch panels that had been quickly installed in Nebraska in the lower part of the body had to be redone. They overlapped and covered rusted sheet metal that needed to be removed. Plus, the lower areas were covered with a thick layer of plastic filler. If I was going to invest a lot of time and money building the car, the bodywork needed to be done correctly. So, one area at a time, I stripped everything down to bare metal cut out the rusted areas, and butt welded the patch panels into place. I bought a MIG (metal inert gas) welder for this project because it used lower, concentrated heat than the oxy acetylene gas welder I had used on my previous '37 Ford project. After tacking panels into place, small alternating weld beads were laid down to minimize warping. After completely welding a panel, the weld beads were ground down and the sheet metal worked with a hammer and dolly to shape it. Sometimes a little shrinking of the metal was required. In this process a spot is heated to a dull red with a torch and then quenched with cold water. This may have to be repeated until the panel conforms to the desired shape. Sometimes you might shrink too much, and the panel had to be worked with a hammer and dolly again. It is amazing how metal reacts to heating, shrinking and working. It is an acquired skill that cannot be taught in

1932 Coupe. Working patch panels and lower body rust. Most of the time-consuming work was in restoration of the body.

The Deuce Coupe that Stole My Heart

Left rear quarter panel being repaired. No patch panels were available so everything had to be hand fabricated.

a classroom. I wouldn't exactly call myself an expert on the subject, but my work was certainly satisfactory.

As I worked my way around the lower body, I came to an area in the rear that required special attention. The left rear corner contained rust, but it was evident that it also had been hit in this corner at some point in its life. A couple of beauty lines come together here that had to be duplicated. There are no patch panels made for this area, so every square inch of it had to be hand formed which is very time consuming. This is why aftermarket fiberglass bodies became so popular so quickly. They are less work than salvaging original old bodies. During this time there were also manufacturers of steel bodies coming on line to supply the demand. These are beautiful, expensive reproductions of the original cars with fresh, clean sheet metal. I was determined that I wanted to restore an original. I've been told that there are many more 1932 Fords on the road today than there were back in the day because of all the reproductions.

I was working on the car one day and a postal delivery truck was in the neighborhood. The truck drove past our driveway, stopped, and then backed up. The postal worker got out of his truck and approached me. I stopped whatever I was doing and we started talking. The guy turned out to be a gentleman by the name of Doug Metheny. He admired my project car so much that it inspired him to start building one for himself. He eventually selected a fiberglass body and worked with a hot rod builder in West Hartford to complete his car. Doug became a good friend, and we maintain our friendship to this day. I have met many nice men and women in the hot rod hobby, and it becomes a fraternal thing where everyone shares help, information, and comradeship.

CHAPTER 10

I continued to work on the '32 coupe project. I worked on the car almost every day, making progress one step at a time. After all the lower panels had been welded in, it was time to work on the floor. To lift the body off the chassis, I built two frames out of two-by-fours and two-by-eights. The car was jacked up, wood frames installed, body unbolted from the frame and chassis lowered to the ground.

This suspended the body in a position that I could access all areas of the floor. Part of the floor restoration process was to weld a clearance bump over the vicinity of the rear end pumpkin (which is the ring and pinion gear). This clearance was necessary for full suspension travel to prevent the rear end from contacting the underneath side of the floor. After completion of the floor, the body was reattached to the chassis and the car lowered back to ground level.

At this point in the restoration process, I started work on the rear wheel wells. There is a beauty line that goes

Wood gantry to lift coupe body off chassis. This was necessary to gain access to the underside of the car for floor repair.

along the upper edge of the wheel well. When the fenders are installed, this beauty line follows the contour of the fender. There was a lot of rust in this area which was exposed after sand blasting. This area required careful attention and time-consuming effort to weld new metal into the complex feature. When it was finished, I etched the area with an acid that converted any remaining rust into black oxide. This was done to both inside and outside surfaces. The outer surfaces were painted with automotive primer and the inner surfaces coated with a thick fish oil base primer. I almost gave up on the project a couple of times at this point because of all the work, but I am glad I persisted.

I now turned my attention to the upper portion of the

Floor bump to provide clearance to rear end pumpkin. The big nine-inch Ford rear end needed some extra room for full travel.

body. Fortunately, there was a patch panel available for the cowl vent surround. This area was so badly rusted that it needed to be replaced with new metal. There is a drain hole in this surround that must have been plugged and water sat in the recesses, causing the rust. I was able to use the original vent door after a little sand blasting and weld repair. Cowl vents were ingenious. If you opened it up on a hot day using the handle under the dashboard, air would dump on to your lap and through the passenger area. If you opened the side windows and the rolled down rear window, a nice flow of air would pass through the car to keep you cool... Poor man's air conditioning!

Next, the trunk lid. I took it to a local sand blaster to thoroughly clean it and expose any rust. It turned out to be a big mistake having this guy blast the trunk lid because

New cowl vent surround tack welded in place. Fortunately a patch panel was available for this repair.

he used such high intensity pressure that it warped the sheet metal badly. Maybe it wasn't such a good idea to use a so called 'professional' after all. It took a lot of work to straighten it out. The trunk lid has a double wall, so it was almost impossible to use a hammer and dolly to work the metal. I had to drill holes in the outer skin and use a slide hammer to pull the surface back into position. Also, It needed a lot of shrinking because metal had been stretched by the intense blasting. Restoration of the trunk lid was very time consuming, but I persisted and was finally rewarded with a completed unit.

I needed an engine, transmission, and driveshaft for my project car. This is when I turned to a friend, Glenn Sinon, who had a 1947 Ford coupe. Glenn was going to pull the 350 cubic

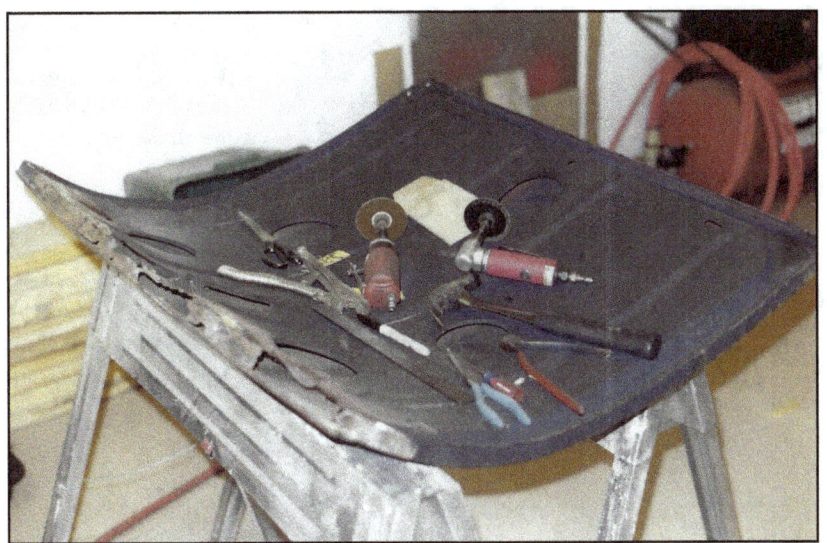

Trunk lid being prepared for new metal. A complex repair because of sand-blast warping and double wall construction.

inch Chevy engine from the '47 and replace it with a new crate motor. Because I was watching the budget very closely on my car project, I opted to get a used engine instead of a new one. I drove Glenn's '47 with the old drive train in it and was satisfied that it would fit my needs. I helped him pull the engine and transmission at a shop in Middletown, Connecticut. I loaded it into the back of my pickup truck and took it to our house. I purchased an engine lift and unloaded the motor onto an engine stand and the transmission on to a four-wheeled dolly. The engine was just a stock motor of about 275 horsepower, but it had a nice four-barrel carburetor sitting on a polished aluminum intake manifold. After some cleaning and painting, the engine was looking pretty good. The transmission also

Top & Middle: Engine and transmission cleaned and detailed. Transplanted power train from a friend's hot rod.

Bottom: Engine complete and dressed with components. They sure look pretty when they are all cleaned up and detailed.

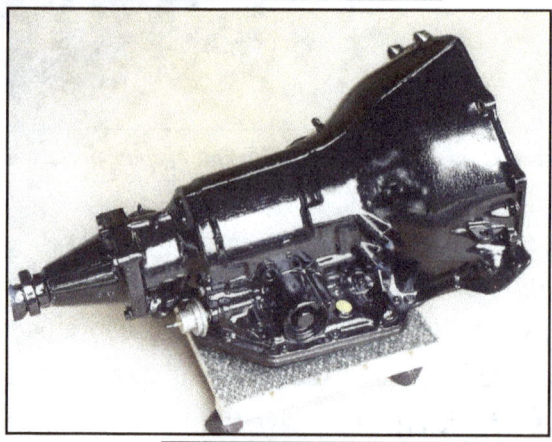

The Deuce Coupe that Stole My Heart

looked brand new.

To install a Chevy engine in one of these old cars, the firewall needed to be recessed about three or four inches for clearance. The original four- or eight-cylinder engines were smaller than their more modern Chevy or Ford counterpart. Ford engines were longer than the Chevrolet and required a little bit extra firewall recess. I lifted the 350 Chevy engine into the '32 chassis for a trial fit and determined how much to recesses the firewall. The firewall was cut, and new sheet metal welded into the recess. Multiple trial fits were done to assure adequate engine and rear mounted distributor clearance. I then married the engine to the transmission and installed it into the chassis. I was lucky that this chassis was already set up for a Chevy engine and the frame rails boxed for the increased horsepower. Hotrodders gravitated to the Chevy engine because it was a small, light engine and there was a lot of reasonably priced aftermarket speed equipment available. Now that the engine installation and firewall recess was done, it was time to move on to the next phase of the build.

The '32 car project was interrupted at this point. We had been thinking of buying another house and a new development was just starting by a local builder on a farm nearby. I could certainly use more garage space, and this was the perfect opportunity to make that happen. We had been in our current house for 27 years and had raised our kids here, but it was time to move on. The real estate market was hot. We met with the builder and since we would be the first house in the new neighborhood, we had the pick of the home sites. We chose a lot at the top of the hill overlooking the Connecticut River valley, downtown Hartford, and the Metacomet Ridge, 17 miles to the west. The lot was located on a cul-de-sac in a quiet corner of the development. The site backed up to an old Nike missile base and wooded acreage of town property.

We looked over house plans and selected a two-story traditional design with a two car garage. The plans were modified to include a third car garage that would be heated and well lit. It would be perfect for my car project. The wheels, so to speak, were set in motion and the '32 Ford as well as the roadster would eventually have a new home.

Firewall with cutout for engine clearance and dash panel. All grit blasted and ready for modification and paint.

CHAPTER 11

Our new house was being built, and, since we lived nearby, I checked on the progress every day. I brought a cooler of drinks and snacks to the workers often with the suggestion to only drink the beer after they were finished for the day. In the meantime, I prepared our current house for sale.

I built a signpost out of four-by-four inch wood and painted it white. I had a local sign shop create a metal FOR SALE sign. It was Friday morning when I planted the new post and sign in the front yard. By noon, we had our first inquiry and by Sunday we had a down payment on the house. The problem was that our new house wasn't going to be ready for another three months, so we ended up selling the house to the new owners and renting it back from them for a few months. Now the pressure was on the builder to finish our new house.

When we finally had to vacate our old house, we had

Our new house with third car garage. Finally a well-lit and heated garage to work in to build the hot rod.

everything put in a mover's trailer and held for the next week. In the meantime, we rented a hotel room nearby to have a place to stay. We finally closed on the new house and moved in. The roadster and the coupe were already in the new garages with permission from the builder.

I had the third car garage set up with good lighting, an electrical connection for my 60-gallon compressor, and a gasfired heater installed near the ceiling. After building a work bench, my new shop was good to go. With a new house, there were plenty of projects to tackle and so I didn't get to work on the coupe every day, but I got something done on it at least every week. One of the first things I wanted to do in my new garage was to chop the roof off the coupe. This is another way hotrodders got their race cars to go faster. A lower roof line meant less wind resistance and more speed. A minor chop could consist of lowering the roof line as little as one inch. A radical chop could be five inches or more. After a lot of research, I decided to chop the roof four inches in the front and three and a half in the rear. That would give a slight sloping appearance to the roof which, to my eye, looked proportionately appealing.

There are various ways to build these cars. A highboy is a style where the body sits on top of the frame as original but with no fenders, hence, a fenderless highboy. A lowboy, on the other hand, is a style where the body is lowered or channeled over the frame and, as a result, the overall height is very low. I liked the look of a highboy, but the original roof height was too tall. It reminded me of a telephone booth, so that is why I decided to chop the roof. When a

Coupe before roof chop. This reminded me of a telephone booth because of the tall roof.

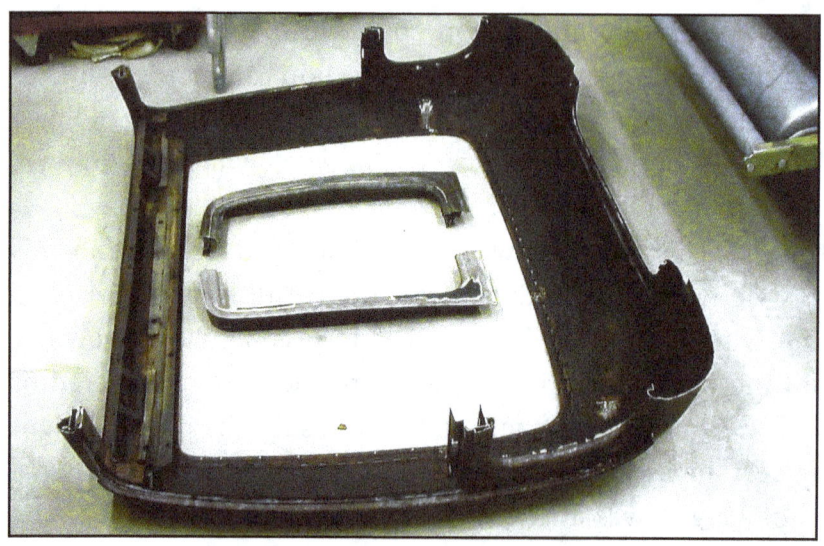

Top: Roof and door parts during chop modification. Lots of work to make the modification look like it grew there.

Bottom: Roof chopped four inches front, three and one-half inches rear.

The Deuce Coupe that Stole My Heart

'A' pillar modification requires lots of cutting and welding. The pillars were laid back five degrees.

'Rear quarter view of coupe just after chop.

roof is chopped, there are two ways to do it. The roof can be sectioned above the doors on each side. The front roof half is moved forward, and the rear half moved aft. The one-inch gap is then filled in with sheet metal. The second method is to lay back the A pillars (windshield posts) and avoid sectioning the roof. I decided on the second method and laid the pillars back five degrees. It sounds easy, but there is a lot of slicing, dicing, and welding to make the modification look like it grew there. I spent a lot of time working on the roof chop. The A pillars were the most challenging.

If the top is chopped, then of course the doors have to be chopped as well. Making the chopped doors fit the door opening is an art. The window openings were cut in

Doors being chopped to match roof line. Very time consuming to make the doors fit properly.

the same manner as the top so that wasn't too much of a problem but getting the door gaps right was a heck of a lot of work. The original '32 Fords had large door gaps mainly because they were driven on unimproved roads resulting in a lot of twisting of the chassis and body. My gaps would be a lot tighter and more consistent than the original. I welded a heavy weld rod on to the edge of the doors and then ground it little by little to make the gaps perfect.

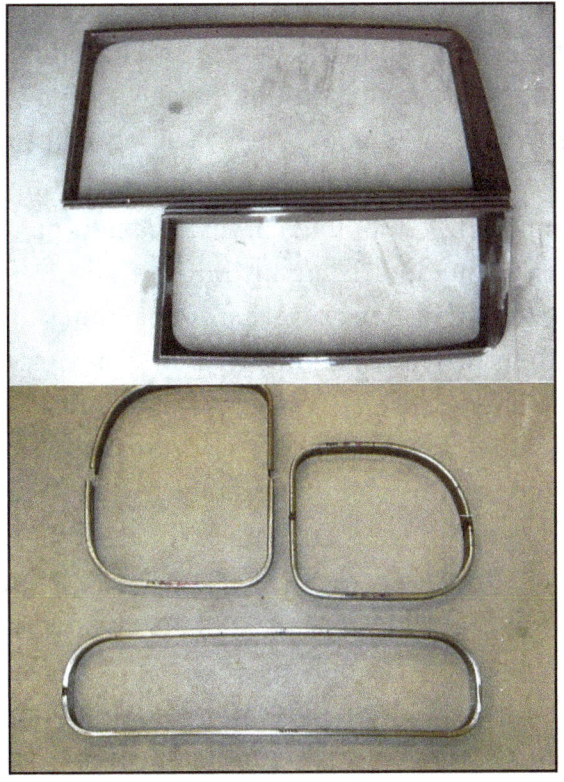

Garnish moldings being modified. Original two-door sedan moldings were cut down to fit the coupe.

After all the welding on the door edges, I adjusted the contour of the doors by using a piece of wood in the door jam and bending the door until it conformed to shape of the opening. Some of these methods are not pretty, but they are simply effective.

After chopping and fitting the doors, the passenger door had a wrinkle in the skin that I could not work out using hammer and dolly or shrinking techniques. I had to replace the entire outer skin from the upper beauty line down to the bottom of the door. I cut out the old skin and formed a new one from fresh metal with a soft faced hammer on a boat cushion on the floor of my garage. I didn't have fancy equipment like an English Wheel, rolling mill or stretcher/shrinker machine so I improvised by taking my time and hand forming the compound curves. The new panel was then welded on to the door using my MIG welder.

Now that the doors were roughed out, it was time to work on the garnish moldings for the inside window openings. This was relatively easy compared to the rest of the chop job. I couldn't find any original or reproduction (repop) door garnish moldings, but I did have a pair of larger sedan moldings that came with the car. I was able to chop them to fit the doors. There were a couple of repop manufacturers making quarter and rear window moldings. One manufacturer was making them out of aluminum, and one out of steel. I went with the steel moldings because they would be easier than aluminum for me to chop and weld. Welding aluminum is an art and I was not good at it. I ordered the three steel moldings and modified them to fit.

The Deuce Coupe that Stole My Heart

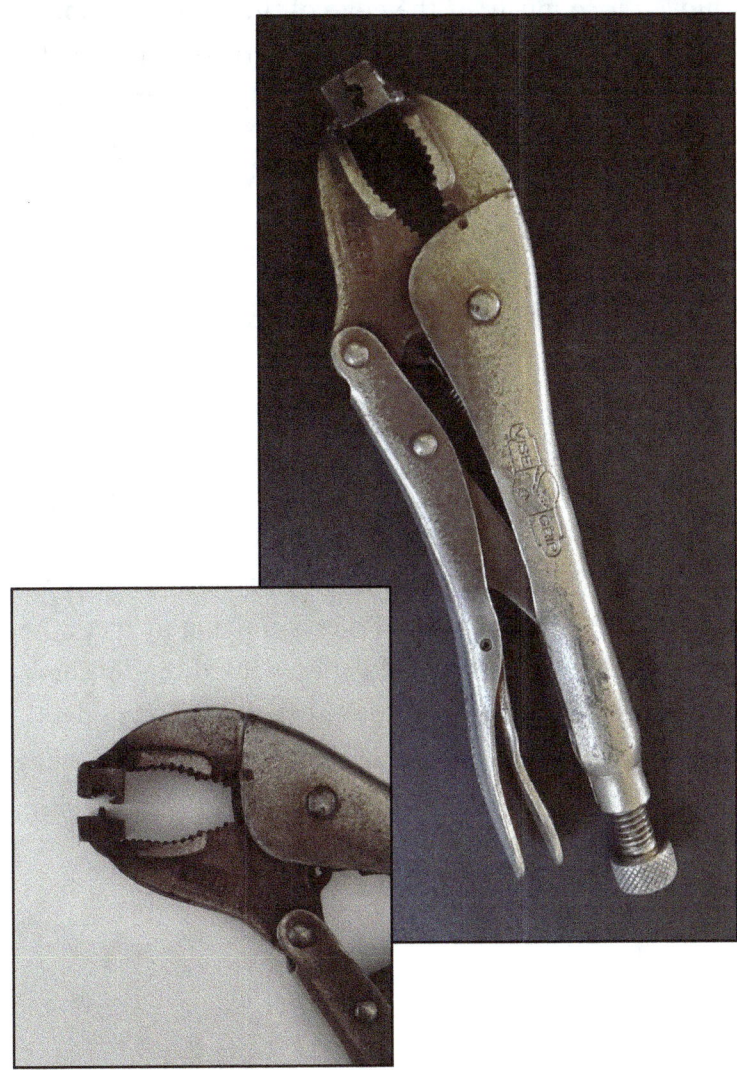

Vise grip with dies to form rain gutter bead. Yankee ingenuity was required to reproduce this feature.

Richard Stoebel

Everything was a new challenge on this car which is why I enjoyed it so much. At the edge of the roof and door openings are water gutters which were also rusted. I drilled out the spot welds holding these in place and took them to a collector car restoration shop in town to see if they could duplicate them. After looking at the parts they declared that they had no equipment or methods that could be used to fabricate the replacements.

Most hotrodders just took these parts off the car and welded the spot weld holes closed. I wanted my car to be as original as possible so I would find a way to fabricate them. After studying the situation, I decided to cut the upper edge off the gutters and weld new metal to the beefier lower part. I fabricated one-inch-long dies to produce the bead along the upper edge. I welded the dies to a pair of vise grip pliers and proceeded to form the bead one agonizing inch at a time. The method was successful, and I spot welded the finished gutters back onto the roof. I was proud to fabricate something that even a professional shop could not do. This was turning into a fun project.

The Deuce Coupe that Stole My Heart

Rain gutter removal and restoration. It was important to me to save this feature on the coupe for originality.

CHAPTER 12

With the engine fitted into the chassis, it was time to fill the recessed opening of the firewall. Fresh sheet metal was welded into place with clearance for the distributor and transmission. This was a fairly easy job, but the engine and transmission had to be put in and taken out several times to accommodate the modification. Once the welding was finished and the welds ground down, it was time to install the front flooring and transmission tunnel.

I had purchased an aftermarket floor shifter and emergency brake handle and bolted them on to the transmission. With that finished, it was time to fabricate the floor. I made the floor out of plywood but skinned the underneath side with steel. I did not want wood exposed on the bottom of the car. The floor also accommodated an opening for the brake master cylinder. Access to the master cylinder was required for topping off brake fluid.

I did not have the machinery to roll curves in sheet

Firewall recess to clear new engine. Several trial fits of the engine and transmission were required during fabrication.

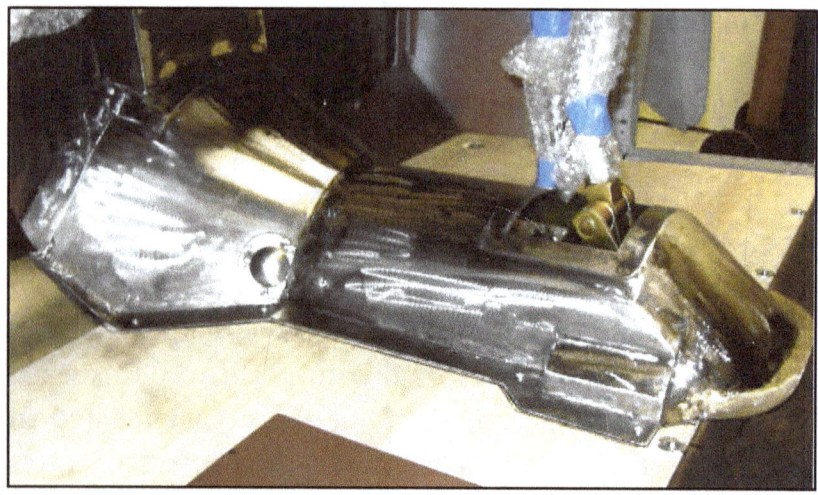

Transmission tunnel fabrication. The telephone pole in front of our house came in handy for the forming process.

metal to fabricate the transmission tunnel, or hump as it was called in the past, so, I simply used the telephone pole out in front of our house to form the shape. Up north we called this Yankee ingenuity. Then the curved section was welded to other pieces of the tunnel and the flanges. I was happy with the finished product. It was, in my estimation, a work of art. It's too bad that it was all going to be covered up by carpeting and floor mats.

When you are building a vehicle from scratch, there are a million details that need to be addressed. At this point in the build, I concentrated on the steering box, column, and wheel. I purchased these components from a variety of hot

Shift lever and emergency brake handle installed during fabrication of the transmission tunnel.

Richard Stoebel

Classic banjo steering wheel from 1937-1939 Ford cars. This iconic steering wheel was a 'must have' for the project. I've always liked the looks of this design.

rod parts supply businesses. When you get into this hobby, you establish the contacts needed to locate all the pieces of the puzzle. Because I was requiring so many parts, UPS and FedEx trucks were beating a path to my door. Packages were arriving daily. It was like Christmas all year round. I got a Vega steering box, a polished stainless-steel column and column drop, and a banjo steering wheel. All these components were fitted to the car and the steering linkage hooked up.

When I aligned the steering system, it was all done with a few measurements and by eye. No front-end specialist

The Deuce Coupe that Stole My Heart

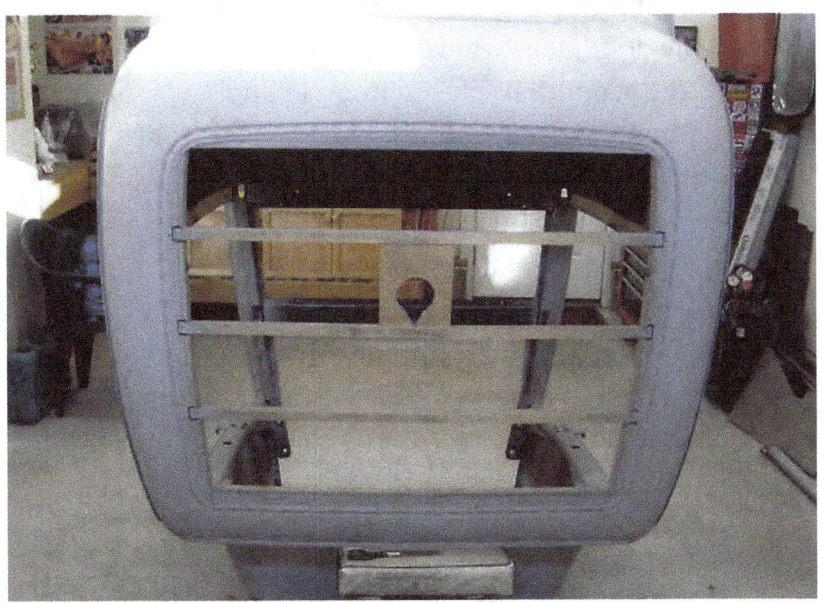

Oak wood roof supports. There was still wood being used for the door jams and roof surround in 1932 Ford cars.

was needed for this simple setup. Caster and camber were determined by the solid front axle and four bar radius rods. Steering wheel centering and wheel toe-in were adjusted by the pitman arm attached to the steering box and the adjustable master and connecting steering rods. This system was certainly much simpler than the independent suspension four-wheel alignment used today. That's why I liked working on these old cars. If you were mechanically inclined, you could do a lot of work on them all by yourself.

A lot of wood frame structure was used in early 20th century cars. In fact, cabinet makers use to build the wood frames and sheet metal workers would attach the metal panels. By 1932, Fords were mostly steel but still had some wood in the door jams, windshield header and roof surround. I bought the wood oak pieces from a supply company that had been making them for years. Of course, since the car had been chopped, I had to also chop the wood door jams to fit. Working with the wood was a lot easier than working with metal so this was done quickly. Metal was attached to the wood using small nails, which was basic stuff.

I purchased a Walker radiator for the car. It was stock height and included an integral air conditioning cooler. I decided to lower the nose of the coupe by one inch. I saw this modification in an article in one of the hot rod magazines and I wanted to incorporate it into the build plan. I returned the original radiator and exchanged it for the same type, but one inch shorter. Once I received the new radiator it was installed and my '32 grille shell was sectioned for clearance over the front frame cross member because of the lower position of the radiator. I also installed an electric cooling fan and shroud.

Now that the radiator and grille shell were installed, I proceeded to section the upper hood halves to match the lowered radiator. I made a pie cut in the hood pieces varying from one inch wide at the front to zero at the rear. I welded the pieces together and dressed the welds, basically doing body work on the inside and outside of the hood. After some reworking of gaps, the hood was sprayed in primer. The modification in my estimation looked pleasing to the eye. Anyone looking at the car could never tell that the front had been lowered.

The Deuce Coupe that Stole My Heart

Sectioning the hood to match lowered radiator and grille shell. The subtle modifications required to custom build a hot rod.

The windshield frame came from another manufacturer of early Ford parts. It was plain steel and stock height. Of course, the frame had to be chopped four inches to match the smaller windshield opening. Then it was sent to the chrome shop for clean, polish, copper base coat, and chrome. Next, it was off to the glass shop for installation of tinted glass. The glass was set in a cushioned waterproof liner. When the windshield was installed, the '32 started to take the shape of a nearly finished car, however there was still a lot of work before it was finished.

Car in primer. After a lot of work the '32 was finally starting to look like a complete car.

CHAPTER 13

I purchased a seat frame from a hot rod shop. It was a stock seat with a handle for forward and back adjustment and another for back tilt. After mocking it up in the car, I discovered that the width was too wide. Once the padding and upholstery was installed, the closed doors would make contact with the seat. How could this happen? It was a stock seat being installed in a stock car.

After taking measurements, I determined that the seat needed to be one inch narrower. I proceeded to make the modification so that it was a perfect fit. I also did this same modification for my friend Doug who had the same problem when he was building a fiberglass version of my car. Primer was now applied to the body, trunk lid, doors, and hood. It was nice to see the car all in one color, even though it was gray primer.

At this point in the build the car needed to be disassembled to work on brake lines, fuel lines and exhaust

Richard Stoebel

Completed chassis with exhaust dump. It was easy to work on the chassis with body removed and everything accessible.

system. Part of the process of building one of these cars is to build it (sometimes multiple times for some components), disassemble it for paint or powder coating, and then put it all back together for the final time. There isn't a rule book for doing this and there are various ways to get the same outcome. Now that the body was removed from the chassis, I had full access to the frame. I started with brake lines. Lines were plumbed from the master cylinder under the floor to the four corners of the car. Hard lines were double flared and then flexible lines installed from the terminal ends of the hard lines to the wheel brake cylinders. Even though this was all going to be hidden once the body was reinstalled, I tried to make the lines as neat as possible. Stainless steel clips were used to attach the hard lines to the frame. Each clip required a drilled and tapped hole in the frame for a machine screw.

    The next thing to be installed was the fuel line that ran from the new reproduction gas tank in the rear to the engine fuel pump up front. The tank I purchased was a stock size steel tank of 11-gallon capacity. There are larger tanks of 14.5 gallons available in steel, stainless steel and plastic, but I opted for the stock size. Again, steel lines were run along the inside frame rail and connected to the mechanical engine fuel pump with a flexible line. Stainless steel clips were used just like for the brake lines. I was getting good at bending and mounting these lines for a professional finish. A dual exhaust system was needed and this would be a little more difficult to fabricate than the brake and fuel lines. I had new ceramic coated headers installed on the engine and decided to ceramic coat the entire exhaust system for longevity. A few six foot long by two-inch diameter pipes were purchased along with a variety of curved sections. Starting with the exhaust pipes that connected to the headers, I worked my way back to where the glass pack mufflers would be attached.

I had seen hot rods with exhaust dumps coming out of the exhaust pipes just downstream of the engine and before the mufflers. These dumps, when uncapped, could allow the engine exhaust to exit without being muffled. I thought it would be a great addition to the exhaust system and this was the time to do it. Uncapped, the '32 would sound like a race car. The forward portion of the exhaust system was suspended from the frame with flexible hangers which were required to absorb engine movement. From the mufflers, it was then up and over the rear end, exiting on either side of the gas tank. It took a lot of cutting and welding to make the pipes follow the path I selected. Clearance was obviously required to the adjacent frame rails, cross members, and suspension components. Once everything was completed, the pipes were disassembled and sent to a local shop for ceramic coating, both inside and out. This exhaust system should last for the life of the car, and maybe well beyond my remaining years.

The emergency brake cable was hooked up at this time. The cable ran from the transmission mounted handle to the rear brakes. It was a pretty straight forward kit, and the cables could be trimmed to length at the rear wheels. The automatic transmission dip stick and fluid fill line was plumbed from the transmission to the firewall. It was easy to do all these installations with the body off the chassis and everything exposed. 1932 Fords were unique in that the firewall was separate from the car body. During assembly, the firewall was installed on the chassis first and then the body lowered over it. A thick rubber gasket was sandwiched in between the two. This was the only year Ford used the separate firewall design. At this time a million other details were attended to while everything was accessible on the chassis. Brackets were welded onto the forward frame rails to attach hood hold down handles. The MIG welder came in handy to burn a deep penetrating weld into the thicker materials of the frame and brackets. I sent the driveshaft that I got with the engine and transmission to a machine shop to shorten it and to weld on a rear U-joint that was compatible with the Ford nine-inch rear end. After modification, the shaft assembly was balanced. It fit perfectly upon installation, and we now had a complete drive train. It was time to disassemble everything for painting and powder coating.

Parts on basement floor. After disassembly for painting, I was amazed at the number of parts that would have to be reinstalled later.

CHAPTER 14

Now was the time to disassemble everything and prepare the components for final assembly. When I finished stripping the chassis, I laid out all the parts on the basement floor and took a picture. I secretly hoped I could remember how they all would go back together! With the frame stripped, it was ready for cleaning, primer, and paint.

To paint all the surfaces, I decided to rotisserie the frame on two engine stands. That way I could get access to all the surfaces and tight spots with the spray gun. I lined the garage with plastic sheets and prepared to spray the gloss black PPG single stage urethane paint. After applying several coats everything was looking good and I was really satisfied with the finished product. It took a lot of work to get to this point.

Next it was time to paint the rear end. I cut some octagonal plywood plates about the size of a tire and bolted them to the axle housing. This made it easy to "roll" the rear

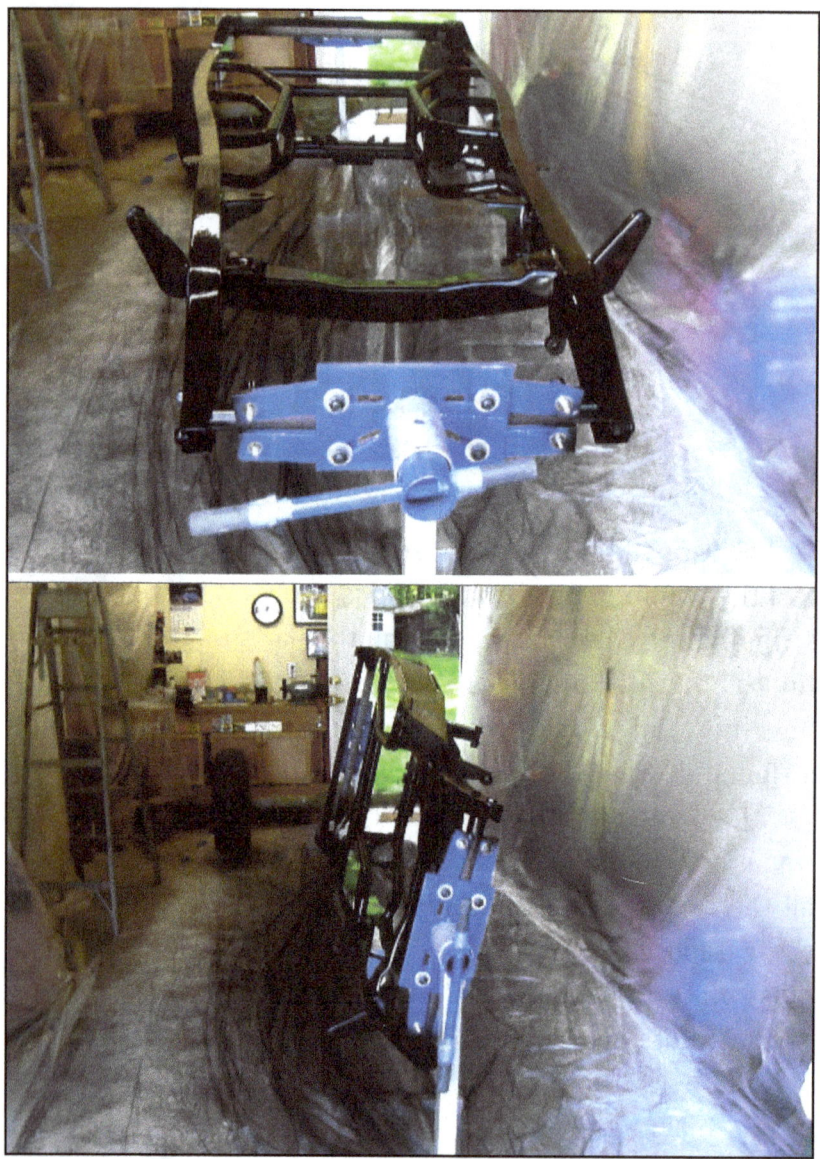

Frame paint with rotisserie engine stands. This was the easy way to paint all the nooks and crannys of the frame.

end outside for primer and paint. I used the same gloss black PPG paint that was applied to the frame.

The four-inch dropped front axle was cast iron. The "drop" was a modification done in the early days of racing to lower the front end of the car for less wind resistance. Another treatment to the axle was to drill holes in the center section to remove weight and allow air to flow through. I think it looked kind of cool. The holes wouldn't affect the strength of the axle since tension and compression loads were all carried by the outer I-beam edges. I laid out the spacing on the center section and began to drill starting with a pilot hole and then a step drill. I drilled all the one-inch diameter holes right on the garage floor. After modification, the axle was sent out for powder coating. I wanted all the suspension components in the front end to have this hard surface coating instead of paint which could chip.

With the rear end and front axle finished, I could start assembly of the chassis. Before I started bolting parts on to the frame, I decided at this point to paint the firewall, dash, gas tank and underneath side of the body. I had seen a picture of the body being painted by simply lifting it up onto the nose of the front cowling. This gave total access to the bottom of the body. After the bottom was painted, two planks of two-by-eight wood were bolted to the underneath side and large casters attached to them. When the body was tipped back to horizontal position, it could now be conveniently rolled around the garage. It would also be handy for transporting the body to the paint shop.

The final body work was done by my friend Glenn Sinon

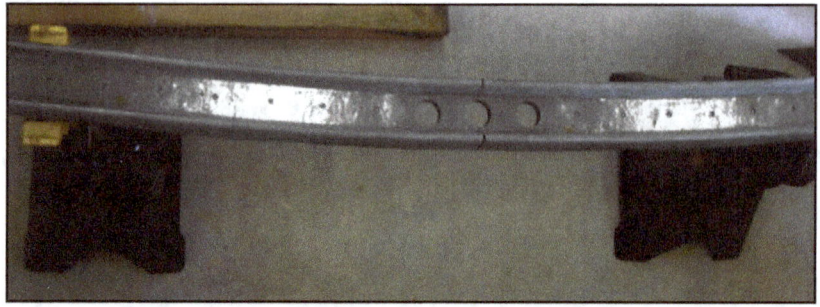

Drilling the front axle. Originally done to remove weight from race cars, I think the looks of a drilled axle is cool.

Painting the nine-inch Ford rearend. I devised the 'wooden wheel' plywood attachments as a way to move and paint all areas of this component.

The Deuce Coupe that Stole My Heart

in West Suffield, Connecticut. Glenn was a master painter and instructor for PPG. He and his dad had all the expertise necessary to bring the coupe to the next level of completion. I had painted the entire car in primer, but these guys would build up the finish so that everything was perfect before applying final paint. I envisioned gloss black for a finish, but after Glen worked on the car for a while, he recommended going with a dull hot rod black, almost like a primer, because the body was far from perfect. If you are going to paint a car gloss black, the surfaces must be perfect. I initially took his suggestion and ordered the paint. Once I got the paint, I did an about face and insisted on going gloss black. We knew this would require many more hours of work, but Glenn finally conceded, and the gloss paint was ordered.

Finished chassis. This was a milestone moment when all chassis parts were painted, coated, polished and reassembled.

Body bottom paint. This made it so easy to gain access to the bottom of the body and to prepare it for rolling around on caster wheels.

The Deuce Coupe that Stole My Heart

Body in spray booth for final finish at a PPG facility in Windsor Locks, Connecticut. All temperature and humidity controlled

The Deuce Coupe that Stole My Heart

CHAPTER 15

Now the body was to be installed on the chassis. To accomplish this, I enlisted the aid of a bunch of friends from the Connecticut Street Rod Association. A promise of coffee and donuts would be waiting for them on this cold spring day.

At the appointed time of 9:00 a.m., my friends started to arrive. I rolled the chassis outdoors and the body was patiently waiting in the garage. With all hands on deck, the body was lifted off its wooden roll around base and onto the chassis. I was the orchestra leader, helping to guide the body over the firewall which was already mounted to the frame. In a few anxious moments, it was done and all of us stood back to admire this beautiful creation. It really was now starting to look like a car.

When the '32 was pushed back into the garage we sipped coffee, munched donuts, and talked about project cars. All these guys had built cars over the years, but it was always a thrill to be part of yet another project.

Because I had previously started the engine in the

Chassis complete and rolled outside for body installation. This would be another milestone day after a lot of work getting to this point.

Mounting body on the chassis. Thanks to my friends, many of whom were from the Connecticut Street Rod Association

chassis, I decided to bring the car to life so the boys could hear it running. I hot-wired the ignition system and fired it up in the garage, much to the delight of the guys. After a minute or so, I shut it down and we all had a toast with our coffee cups. There was still more work to be done to finish the car, but I was well on the way to a finished product.

Over the coming weeks, I worked on various projects including the electrical system. I had bought a Bare Bones wiring kit from the Ron Frances Company. I also had bought a set of Haneline gauges that would fit in the original instrument panel opening. I wanted to make sure the wiring

Car in garage after body installation. Starting to look like a complete car but still with a lot of work to do.

First drive without doors, hood and top material. With electrical work done and fuel in the tank, I just had to take the '32 out for a spin.

was done correctly because after it was covered up it would be very difficult to troubleshoot anything electrical. I called the Ron Frances help line a number of times to get answers to questions I had during the installation. Finally, after three months of working on the wiring system, it was finished.

I was anxious to drive the car! The doors were not final installed yet, and the seat was mocked up in place, but with no upholstery. I decided to take the car out for a joy ride in our neighborhood just for fun. I had not registered or insured it yet but the urge to drive the car beckoned me. So, I fired it up and down the driveway I went. Most neighbors were at work during this weekday morning, so it was the perfect time to drive the '32 for the first time. My friend Doug Metheny was visiting so he took photos to document the occasion. It was nice to finally be behind the wheel of my project car. It was a milestone day!

I needed to get the car registered because I wanted to drive it to a glass shop in Somers, Connecticut. I was referred to a street rod friendly shop in Willimantic, Connecticut for VIN verification. If I had taken an unfinished car like this directly to the DMV (Department of Motor Vehicles), they would have rejected the car for a number of reasons, the main one being that it had no fenders! There was an unwritten rule in Connecticut, and perhaps in most states, that local or state police would not stop you for having a fenderless hot rod unless you were speeding or doing burnouts. Another friend, Brian Snell, agreed to trailer the '32 to Willimantic for the VIN (Vehicle Identification Number) verification. $20 later we were on the way back to my garage with completed paperwork in hand.

After I got the VIN verification, I could now register the vehicle. I had bought a 1932 Connecticut license plate on eBay from a lady out in Montana. It was stamped MP32. After cutting and welding in a letter Y from another license plate, it read MY32. The state of Connecticut allowed antique vehicles to use a license plate of the same year of manufacture as the car, so I went to the DMV with my modified license plate for registration purposes. Connecticut required a front and rear license plate to be displayed at the time. I only had one specialty plate and that would be put on the back of the coupe. The DMV never asked me for a second one! The rear plate must be illuminated, so I fabricated a license plate surround out of brass from a front door kick plate so that it would house two small lights. The surround was hand

Richard Stoebel

Modified license plate and fabricated chrome frame. There is only one license plate like this.

formed over a special wooden buck that I made, then cut out, polished, and sent to the chrome shop. The result was a nice custom frame surrounding the MY32 license plate. No one else had this setup. It was unique to my car.

With the car now registered, I threw a blanket over the bare springs of the front seat and drove it to the glass shop in Somers, taking the back roads just to be cautious. The car had a windshield but no glass in the doors or side and rear windows. I selected a slightly tinted glass and, in a week or so, I would have the car back with all windows installed. I was invited to a cruise night/get together at the shop one evening while the car was being worked on. At that gathering a lot of folks got their first look at my new hot rod.. The '32 was the star of the show! The next project was to fill in the opening in the top of the car. An oak wood kit had been installed and the roof consisted of a perimeter of wood with a series of cross members. The opening was then covered with chicken wire, a layer of wool batting, and a black fabric top which was waterproof just like back in 1932. There were other top kits available from hot rod shops, but I didn't like the look of them because they protruded up higher than the original. I liked the look of the low profile original. The black fabric was tacked to the wood perimeter with small nails. The final step was to nail a metal perimeter strip in place and fill the slot with a rubber seal. The only place currently selling this special metal strip was a shop in Amesbury, Massachusetts. Their strips were made from extruded aluminum as opposed to the original which were made of steel. Since the aluminum was the only kind available, I purchased a number of six-foot lengths.

To form the corner radii, I fabricated two bucks, one for the larger radius at the front, and one for the smaller radius at the rear. The metal had to be heated to anneal it for bending. I used my torch for this step and found out quickly that too much heat would crack the aluminum (hot shortness), and too little would not allow the material to be easily bent. After some trial and error, I was able to find the sweet spot and eventually bent all the radii successfully. The new metal strips were painted and nailed into place. Rubber filler material finished the process. I was very proud of the

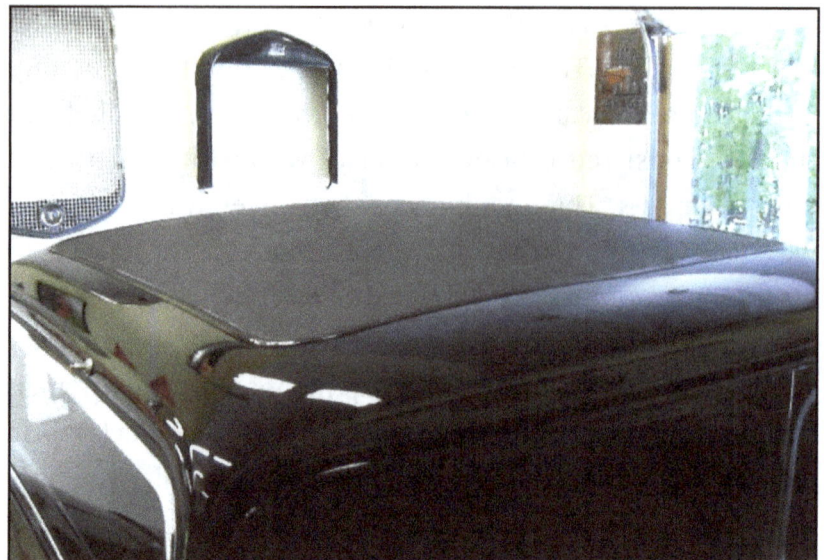

Top material installed just like the original would have been when the car was built in 1932

completed top. The car was really a masterpiece!

My story may be one of the only times where you can follow the whole process of building a hot rod from start to finish with all the dirty details explained. I learned a lot along the way, and I am happy to share that knowledge with you.

CHAPTER 16

It was time for upholstery. I had a friend, Ken Nadeau, in Rockville, Connecticut who had an upholstery shop. He worked on all kinds of cars, but he was partial to old ones and especially old hot rods. Not too many shop owners would let a car owner work with them, but Ken had no problem allowing me to shadow him and help out. I would be the guy to do menial tasks like getting the aluminum sheets that were used as the base panels. I cut the panels to shape and then helped install them when upholstered.

I chose American Beauty Red vinyl material for the coupe. I could have selected leather, but the vinyl looked just as good, and it was a lot cheaper. The material was ordered, and work began. A classic tuck and roll design was chosen for the seat and side panels. Ken also fabricated the floor carpeting and mats from a matching red material. The headliner was installed and the trunk was also fully upholstered. It took a couple of weeks to complete the upholstery work. Ken was

Installing traditional hot rod interior upholstery. Ken Nadeau is a real craftsman and his work is just outstanding.

The Deuce Coupe that Stole My Heart

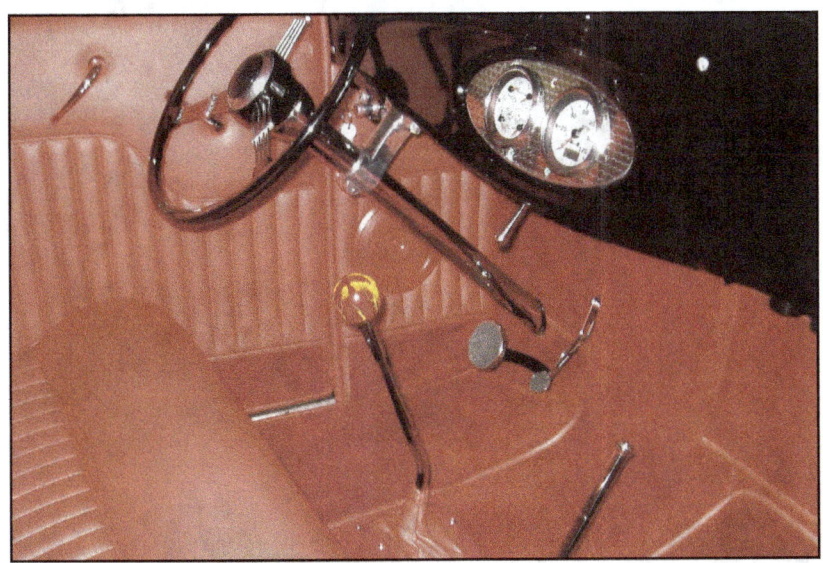

Upholstery complete. The seats, doors, trunk and carpeting finished to perfection in tuck and roll American beauty red vinyl.

a true professional and the work he did on the coupe was phenomenal.

The '32 would now head back to Glenn Sinon's shop for flames. My wife, Brenda, begged me not to chop the roof of the car. I didn't listen to her because I had a picture in my mind of what I wanted the car to look like, so I chopped it anyhow. I also had a vision of painting some traditional flames over the hood of the car. Brenda said she would never ride in the coupe if I did that but, I hoped she would eventually come around and appreciate the car when it was finished. Glenn went to work on the flame job. I wanted the scheme to start off as white (as in white hot) at the nose and trailing off over the hood into yellow and orange. I had a

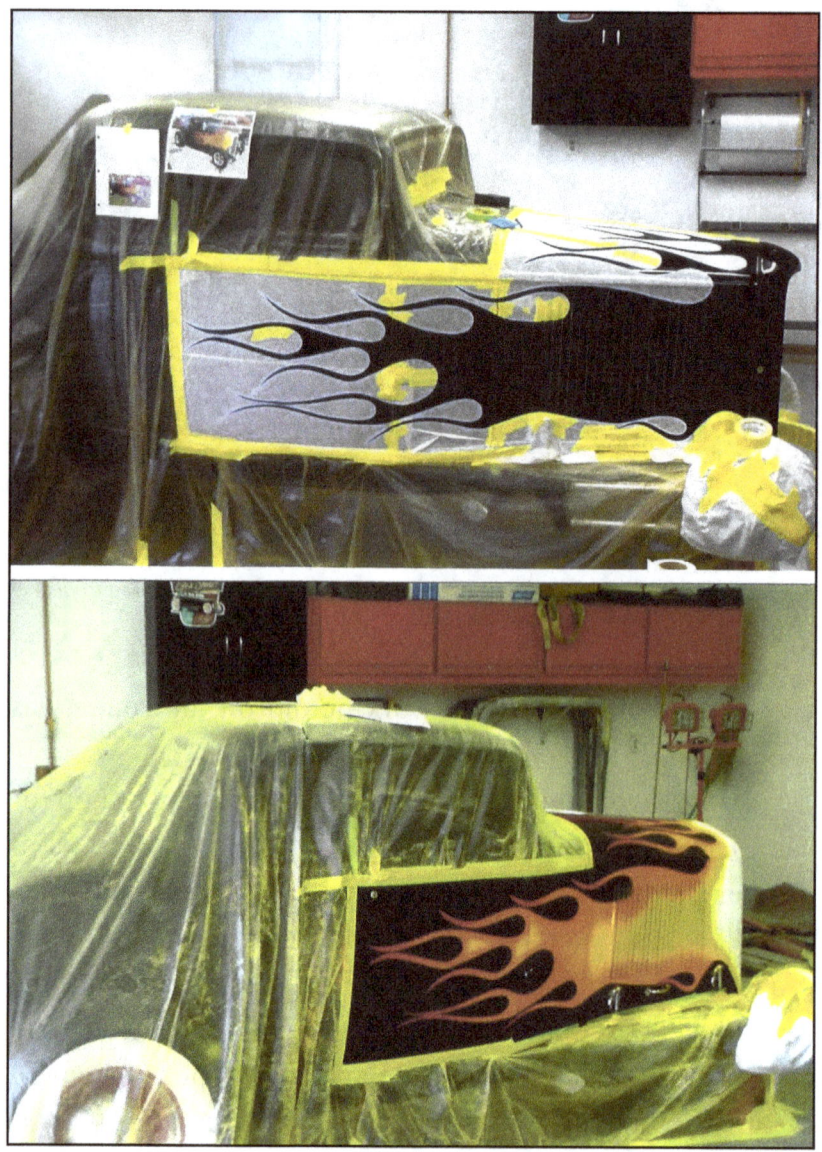

Painting flames. The finishing touch to this project that I had envisioned for this hot rod from the very beginning.

The Deuce Coupe that Stole My Heart

picture from a magazine that we used as a model. The flame job was especially difficult because it had to be masked off over the louvers of the hood sides. The hood consisted of 20 louvers. The early Ford flathead V8 initially had overheating problems. Later, 1932 production models increased the number of louvers to twenty-five to help cool the engine.

After the flame pattern was carefully masked off and spray painted, it was time for the finishing touch. Blue pin striping was added to the edges of the flames by Charlie Decker, known as the one-armed bandit. Charlie had a prosthetic right arm and he used this to steady his left arm and hand while applying the pin striping. Charlie's work was fantastic. He even talked me into pin striping a pattern on the rear trunk lid. It is signed "bandit."

After the flame job was completed at Glenn's shop, on the way home I headed to my first cruise night with the car. Mark's Classic car night in East Granby, Connecticut attracted some 250 specialty and exotic cars on a good night. The coupe got a lot of attention because it was new to the cruise night circuit. I didn't win a trophy, but driving on the way out I overheard a young lady remark that she'd like to be a hood ornament on my car. I responded that would be OK, but she'd have to take all her clothes off. I didn't hear her response, but I left the show feeling like I had just gotten the "Best of Show" award.

Now that the car was complete, I started to think of how I could show it off. Local cruise nights were fun, and I earned a bunch of awards going to them, but I thought it

Richard Stoebel

Pinstriping by the 'Bandit.' I could not do pinstriping if my life depended on it. I just have to admire a real artist like Charlie Decker doing his thing.

might be nice to have the car featured in one of the national magazines. I had a subscription to *Street Rodder* magazine at the time so I contacted Brian Brennan, the editor, to see if he would be interested in my 1932 Ford. He got back to me and requested some photos of the car. After his review, he put me in touch with one of the contributing photographers, Chuck Vranas, who eventually would take photos and write the feature article. Chuck waited until evening for the photo shoot because he liked the light at that time of day. He used a digital camera from a distance with a telephoto lens to capture the images that would be used in the article.

The article was published in the March 2011 copy of *Street Rodder* magazine and it was entitled "Homespun Hot Rod." This was like hitting the lottery for a big win to have your car featured in a national magazine. As any proud builder would do, I bought a bunch of copies of the magazine at the local bookstore. I had hit the big time!

About this time, I got the itch to show the car at national shows. I purchased a brand new 20-foot-long closed trailer. Delivery from Indiana was included in the price, and it arrived a couple of weeks later just in time for the summer show season. Because my light duty Dodge pickup truck could not haul a trailer of this size, I borrowed my son's F250 diesel-powered truck. I had an electric brake control system installed in his truck and I had the local Ford dealer inspect the brakes to make sure it was in good working order. I did not want to lose control of the truck and trailer, and destroy my new hot rod on my trips to the national events.

I could have, and probably should have, just driven the car to the upcoming nationals. I knew the car would make it, but I wasn't sure I had the stamina to spend all those hours on the road dodging potholes and driving in rainy conditions. After my eight years of work on the '32, I just wanted to protect my investment and take the easy way to the shows.

My first trip was to the National Street Rod Association (NSRA) meet in York, Pennsylvania. I had been there before but without entering a show car. My son, Brett, accompanied me on one of those trips. I recall that we arrived late at the hotel, and even though we had a reservation, we got the last room available. It reeked of cigarette smoke. When we complained, the manager came to the room and sprayed it heavily with an air freshener. The room still smelled but we were stuck here for the night. All the local hotels for miles around were full. We had no choice.

This trip with the '32 Ford would be different. I booked into a classier hotel and arrived early. The car was shown over the weekend and got a lot of attention. Other than a couple of rainstorms (it always rains in York) it was a nice weekend with friends. About 3,000 cars come to this event. It is huge. I didn't win any awards, but I did have the car inspected by the Michigan Street Rod folks and garnered a NSRA safety twenty-three award which meant the car met all safety standards. It was nice talking to people and getting compliments on my new car. At the end of the weekend, the '32 was secured in the trailer and hauled back to

The Deuce Coupe that Stole My Heart

Street Rodder *magazine feature article. This is like hitting the lottery when you have your car featured in a national magazine.*

Connecticut. I arrived safely back home and planned for my next excursion to the Syracuse, New York nationals.

CHAPTER 17

I made hotel reservations for the upcoming Syracuse Nationals sponsored in part by Meguiar's, the car polish folks. I met Barry Meguiar and had our picture taken with him at the Grand National Roadster show in Pomona, California a few years earlier. Barry had a television show called *Car Crazy*. He featured me and my 1932 Ford in one video segment of the show. I was always grateful for him doing that. It was time to hit the road again and head for upstate New York.

I submitted coupe pictures for possible consideration for the Gene Winfield award. Gene was a famous builder specializing in custom cars. The winner would take home $10,000 with five additional prizes of $1,000 each. My '32 was selected to be in the running for the awards, but it did not win any of the big money prizes. I was up against professional builders and Gene leaned more towards heavily modified cars instead of traditional ones. However, it was

Richard Stoebel

still an honor to be considered for the monetary prizes.

After a weekend in upstate New York, it was back to Connecticut to prepare for the next show in Poughkeepsie, New York. The Goodguys East Coast Nationals was the last show that I would attend of the big three car shows in the Northeast for the summer. It was fun going to these shows, but it was also a lot of work. I wanted to give my '32 Ford some national exposure while the car was new and fresh. My good friend, Brian Snell, and I trailered our hot rods up to Poughkeepsie for the weekend. I don't think we had hotel rooms, because, as I recall, we just slept in our trailers in sleeping bags. This was a low budget trip. After the weekend, the coupe garnered no trophies but ended up being featured in an issue of the *Goodguys* magazine which was commendable.

The trip back home was uneventful except the F250 dripped transmission fluid and left a trail on the driveway when I got home. I had to fix this problem before returning the truck to my son, so it was back to the Ford dealer in Glastonbury to fix the leak. The transmission was removed, seals replaced, and the transmission reinstalled in the truck. I wanted to give the truck back to my son in good condition. I appreciated him loaning it to me. Of course, I had loaned my Dodge pickup to him during this time only to learn that one of my grandsons was taught to say "Ewwwwww, a Dodge!" I get no respect, not even from a grandson.

Now that my travel days to national events with the coupe were over, I put the trailer up for sale. As it turned

The Deuce Coupe that Stole My Heart

out, I ended up selling it for slightly more than I paid for it to a guy with a couple of Pontiac Solstices. The trailer owed me nothing. Now it was back to just local car shows and cruise nights. One of the big shows in our area was the Manchester Cruisin' on Main in August. This is a one day show with hundreds of vintage cars, trucks, and custom vehicles. The show is always on a Sunday and takes up the entire Main Street in town with food vendors and entertainment. I drove my new '32 coupe to the show and my wife drove our 1930 roadster. It was a beautiful day for the show. It just doesn't get any better than this.

The show ran from 9:00 a.m. to 3:00 p.m. Afterwards, we had invited all our hot rod friends and neighbors back to the house for a party. We had enough beer and hot dogs and hamburgers for an army. Good friend and fellow

Coupe and roadster at 'Cruising on Main' show. Manchester, CT. I drove the coupe and my wife drove the roadster to this show.

car enthusiast, Bruce Baldyga, brought his bluegrass band to entertain us. It was a glorious afternoon and evening. Dozens of hot rods were parked in the driveway and cul-de-sac in front of our house. It had been a fun day with great friends. We tried to duplicate this event the following year with the premise that if the car show goes on, rain or shine, the party would go on also. As (bad) luck would have it, scattered showers were forecast for the day, but the show was not canceled. People with really nice cars were not going to show up in the rain. Because of this our party had a poor turnout. We had a lot of beer left over. Did you know that beer never really goes bad? We were going to test that theory over the coming months.

During the winter months, usually February, the Frank Maratta Auto Show is held in the Hartford, Connecticut area. For many years it was held in the Armory in downtown Hartford but it grew too big for that venue. This year it was being held at the Connecticut Expo Center and I was invited to show the '32 coupe. I had a friend trailer the car to the Expo center. I could have driven it there but with the winter snow, slush, and salt on the roads I decided to use the trailer. We got the car there on Friday morning and started to set up at my assigned space. Stanchions and velvet rope were rented from Taylor Rental, and I had a custom sign made to describe the details of the car. I borrowed a large area rug from a friend to put underneath the car. I was quite proud of my display.

The weekend show drew a lot of people. By this time of year, most people were sick of winter weather and seeking a

The Deuce Coupe that Stole My Heart

Custom coupe display sign. I commisioned this sign for display purposes at outdoor and indoor car shows.

place to go to throw off the winter doldrums. The timing was perfect for this event. After a long weekend, the coupe was awarded a "Best of the Best" trophy and it was time to pack up and go home. Our 1930 Ford roadster had also garnered this trophy some years prior. I still have those two trophies on display today in my garage man cave. These shows are a lot of fun but also a lot of work. It's very gratifying to display something to the public that you made with your own hands.

The '32 would now sleep for the remainder of the winter in the garage until spring and summer arrived. The season for driving these classic cars in New England is cut short by winter when the roads are covered with salt, snow, and ice. Come on springtime!

Best of the best trophies. Both the roadster and coupe garnered trophies at the indoor Frank Maratta show in Hartford.

CHAPTER 18

What's better than having a hot rod? Having two, of course! The question was always "which one should I drive today, the 1930 Ford rumble seat roadster or the 1932 Ford coupe?" What a problem to have. As it turned out, I liked both cars because I had so much time invested in building, maintaining, and, repairing them. I also discovered that I enjoyed building them more than I did driving them. As a result, not a lot of miles were being logged on either car. But the cars were there for me any time I got the urge to drive. We owned both cars outright and owed no money on them.

About this time in our lives, I had been retired for a couple of years and my wife, Brenda, was about to retire. We had always talked about living down south to get away from the winter weather and maybe this was the time to do it. Towards the end of the year, we decided to travel to Florida and check it out. Brenda used the holiday week she had off from work and a couple of weeks of vacation she had remaining just for this trip. We drove south and got to the Sunshine State in two days. We had spent time on the East Coast of Florida years ago when I was working for Pratt & Whitney but never spent any time on the West Coast. Our first stop was in Naples on the Gulf of Mexico. This was near the southern tip of Florida and the Everglades were just inland from there.

Coming this far south from New England in December was a real eye opener. It was hot and it was humid. We sat next to the hotel pool in the evening with a bottle of wine for a while but soon retreated to our air-conditioned hotel room. It was going to take some time getting acclimated to the tropical climate. After a couple of days in the area, we headed north along the Gulf coast and up to the Tampa and St. Petersburg area. We were driving along the coast hoping to see beaches and gulf water but all we saw were high rise hotels and condominiums blocking the view. Traffic was so heavy, and we wondered where the heck everyone was going at two o'clock in the afternoon. We didn't like the area with all of it's traffic congestion, so it was time to move on.

We headed further north to Spring Hill near Weeki Wachee Springs. We had some friends from Connecticut living in a retirement community there and so we paid them a visit. The area was nice, but it was older and did not have the amenities and activities that interested us. Route 19 nearby was always congested with traffic. We began to think that this area was not suitable for our retirement dreams, and we should continue our search for the perfect retirement location. Then it was off to The Villages in Central Florida

The Deuce Coupe that Stole My Heart

located a half hour south of Ocala and an hour north of Orlando. As it turned out this is where we ended up building our dream house in this growing retirement community.

After we closed on our new Florida home, we spent three months there the next winter. The following winter we spent five months. We still had our house in Connecticut, and we only intended to be in Florida each year for a few months. During our third winter in Florida, we spent seven months there and knew it was time to sell the house up north. If we were going to live in Florida full time, we needed a bigger house and more garage space for the hot rods. We found our second house in The Villages online, put a deposit on it, and began the transition to that 'forever home.' Our first house in The Villages was sold in one day. The market was really hot in this retirement community.

The first hot rod to be transported to Florida was the roadster. Good friend, Bruce Baldyga, was coming to Florida with an empty trailer to pick up an old truck in Tampa that he had just purchased. We struck up a deal with him to transport the roadster to our new Florida home. The car arrived safely and was tucked away in our new garage.

We spent three months preparing our Connecticut house for sale and decided to sell it on our own, avoiding realtor commission. We had sold our previous house in Connecticut on our own, so we had confidence we could do it again with this house. It wasn't long before we had multiple offers and a deal was made with the most viable buyer.

We contracted a collector car transport company to

Our first Florida home on Ashwood Run in The Villages. Not enough room for hot rods, but that would change in the future.

Our second Florida home on Lake Ridge Drive in The Villages. Now we would have enough room to house the roadster and coupe at our full time home.

take the coupe to Florida. It was loaded into a closed trailer and on its way within a week. It would be received in Florida by a man we hired to watch our house. The transition was completed without incident, and we now had both hot rods in Florida. After closing on our Connecticut house, we jumped into the Acura RL we had at the time and headed south. We still laugh to this day about that trip. The RL was filled with a lot of our worldly possessions including money, jewelry, guns, ammunition, and liquor. As we were traveling through the night, my wife was taking a turn at the wheel. I glanced over at the speedometer and saw the number 80. My response was "You might want to dial it back a little. If we get into an accident or get stopped by the highway patrol, we'll have a lot of explaining to do. We might even end up in jail."

Luckily, we made it to Florida without incident. It was

Transporting the coupe to Florida in a first class enclosed trailer. These professionals really know how to move a car across the country.

nice to see both hot rods in the garage when we arrived. A few days later the moving van showed up with our furniture. I had made custom boxes for neon signage that I had up north as well as other memorabilia that I could eventually display in my new garage man cave.

Our new garage was an oversize two-car layout with a third golf cart space. I purchased four hydraulic lifts which could be placed under each wheel of a car. Pumping the foot activated lever of each lift raised the car so that it could be easily rolled around. These lifts were used to relocate the roadster into the golf cart portion of the garage. Now we had room for our Acura RL, two hot rods and golf cart parked perpendicular to the coupe. Everything fit as planned. I laugh at the notion that if we had a six-car garage, I would probably fill it to the brim with stuff. Such is the nature of a car collector.

Our Acura RL. My wife loved this car for its luxury and handling. We used this car to relocate to Florida with all of our prized possessions.

CHAPTER 19

We were now full-time residents of Florida. When we started spending more than six months a year in Florida, we applied for residency which allowed us to avoid the state income tax in Connecticut. Florida had no state income tax and that saved us at least $7,000 a year. When our house sold up north, we saved another $20,000 a year on taxes, utilities, and upkeep. That is the benefit of living down south, and especially in the Sunshine State.

As we got everything in order at our new house, I started to customize the walls of my man cave garage. My neon signs were strategically hung and a couple more were purchased to fill in the voids. I had one wall dedicated to automobile memorabilia and another to aviation. Since I joined the radio control airplane club, my planes were hung on the aviation wall. I no longer had my car building equipment like compressor, pneumatic tools, MIG and gas welding outfits. I had given those to my son. My car building days were over

Garage with hot rod memorabilia and neon signs. The 'man cave' was starting to come to life with a gas pump and collectibles.

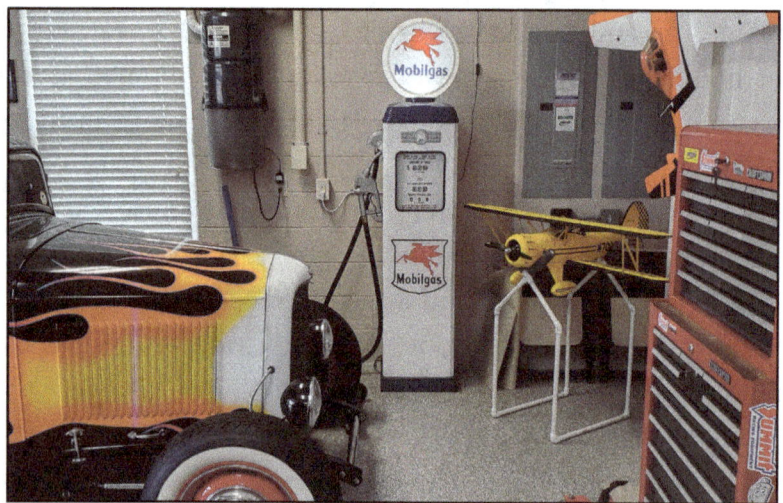

Garage with Deuce Coupe and gas pump. The 'man cave' was starting to look good and a nice place to hang out with friends.

except for light maintenance on my two hot rods.

The nice thing about Florida is that collector cars can be driven year-round. There would be no more winter storage which could last up to five or six months. In fact, winters down south are the ideal time to attend cruise nights and car shows. Summers in Florida are hot and humid, and the heat can be oppressive at times. In Connecticut, a heat wave was declared when two or more days exceeded ninety degrees. In Florida, the whole summer is a heat wave! That's what air conditioning and swimming pools are for.

The roadster was running a little rough and hesitated during acceleration, so I contracted a local performance shop in Ocala to rebuild the carburetor and switch over from a points distributor to electronic ignition. I had rebuilt carburetors in the past but was too busy with fun activities now to do it so I just decided to farm it out. I had put electronic ignition into my coupe distributor and thought it was time to update the roadster as well.

Upon completion at the hot rod shop, I drove the roadster home and then drove it occasionally around The Villages. I don't think I had put more than fifty miles on it when the engine failed to start, and I smelled something burning. The new Pertronix distributor had failed. The car was towed back to the shop where another replacement electronic distributor was installed. Long story short, the distributor failed once again, and the car had to be towed. I insisted that the shop revert back to a points type distributor. They had supposedly thrown out my original distributor. I regret I didn't ask for it to be saved, so I had to purchase a new one. This whole ordeal cost me upwards of $1,000 but I did end up with a rebuilt carburetor and new ignition system including distributor, spark plugs, and wires. I never dealt with this performance shop again and they were probably glad not to see me again.

I had to replace bushings in the front four bar radius rods, but other than that all the maintenance I did on the roadster was oil changes and some new tires. After having owned the roadster for 20 years, it was time to move on. The car still looked and drove good, but it was time for a refresh. I wasn't using the car very much and it was taking up garage space. The decision was made to consign it for sale at Gateway Classic Cars in Orlando. These folks advertised nationally and internationally. After advertising the roadster locally, I was just getting lowball offers. I bought it years ago for $25,000 plus shipping from California. I had put some money into it, including the exhaust system, soft top, and rumble seat. If I could get $39,000 out of it, I would be a happy camper.

Gateway recommended that we have a detailer go over the car to make it look its best. We met with the specialist, and he tried several types of polish on the car in increasing intensity. The thirty-six year-old acrylic enamel responded to the treatment, and we contracted to have the detailing done. When the car was completed, I was amazed at the result. The roadster shone like a jewel.

Subsequent advertising by Gateway included a video and over a hundred pictures of the car. Within six weeks, we had

Roadster for sale at Gateway Classic Cars in Orlando. After 20 years of owning this car it was regretably time to move on.

more than 1,600 hits on the Gateway website with a number of collectors following the bidding. Gateway advertised the car at $51,000 which I found excessive for a hot rod Model A Ford, but a bid finally came in at $42,500. The car was ultimately sold to someone in Ohio. We got our asking price out of it and Gateway got their 12.5% commission. This was a great way to sell a car and I recommend it to anyone buying or selling a collector car.

Now we had an open space in our garage. The plan all along was to get a personal car for Brenda. She had shared the family car which was now a Cadillac SRX for many years. I searched the internet for a car for her, looking for a BMW. We had owned a Ford, Dodge, Pontiac, Acura, Mercedes, and

Cadillac in the past, but never a Beemer. My search found a low mileage one in California. It was a pearl white 2018 230i soft top convertible and had just come off lease. It only had 10,400 miles on it. After a little negotiating, the car was purchased and shipped to us in Florida. It took us a couple of weeks to get the car registered because of a paperwork snafu, but we finally got it done. The light beige interior was perfect for the hot climate we now lived in. You definitely would not want to have a car in Florida with a black interior, especially a convertible. You'd burn your butt and the back of your legs off!

After registering the BMW, it was problematic that the driver's seat was too low for my wife. She is just a cute little five-foot gal and Beemers intentionally positioned the driver to lower the center of gravity (CG) of the car. We tried to contract a local foreign car repair shop to raise the seat, but after several attempts to work with them, we abandoned that approach. We found a riser kit online from a seller in the United Kingdom. It was purchased and sent to us. The kit consisted of four steel blocks about one and a quarter inches tall and four longer attachment bolts. Between my wife and me, we successfully installed the kit and were now good to go. We didn't need a repair shop. This is not rocket science. We could do this modification ourselves. A specialized license plate was also purchased for this car. It reads "NO.1 MAMA."

The Deuce Coupe that Stole My Heart

Our 2014 Cadillac SRX. We purchased this car from a dealer in Sarasota, Florida. It only had 5,000 miles on it.

Brenda's license plate, No.1 Mama. Of course we had to personalize the Beemer with a specialized marker to make it her own.

Brenda's BMW 230i convertible. It was time for my wife to have her own car again. The Beemer came from California and only had 10,400 miles on it

CHAPTER 20

Now that the roadster had been sold and Brenda's BMW was occupying the void in the garage, I could concentrate on maintaining the '32 coupe. I had installed an Optima gel cell battery in this car because the battery was located behind the passenger's seat, and I did not want fumes from a lead acid battery polluting the interior of the car. These gel cell batteries lasted six years in a Connecticut climate but only three years in the heat and humidity of Florida. For this reason, the battery is maintained with a trickle charger connected to it while sitting around in my garage. Many golf carts in our retirement community are battery powered, but from my experience I would only own a gas-powered cart. Maybe the new lithium-ion batteries will fare better in this climate than old lead acid ones.

Long term storage of gasoline is problematic because the Ethanol (usually 10%) in it absorbs water. For that reason, I always use the appropriate amount of Sta-Bil stabilizer treatment in the gas tank of my hot rod, and, I always use ninety-three octane gasoline for good performance. The stabilizer claims that it can prevent gum and varnish buildup for a period of up to two years. It also claims that it absorbs water. A good rule of thumb is to use a gas stabilizer if your vehicle sits for thirty days or more. After the treatment is added to a full tank of fuel (prevents condensation) it is best to run the engine for a minimum of five minutes to circulate the stabilized fuel into the carburetor or fuel injectors. I have used this product for years on snow blowers, pressure washers, golf carts and cars with great results.

Now that I am down to just one hot rod, the '32 Ford coupe, I take it out occasionally to run it around the neighborhood or take it to the local cruise night. I have a California Cover for the coupe, but I never use it because I like to look at the uncovered car in the garage. I save the cover for a situation where I may get caught in the rain.

If the car sits for a while, I use a California Car duster to remove surface contaminants. The duster is impregnated with wax which picks grime up, not push it around. After the duster, I then use a detailing spray wax and a soft microfiber cloth to polish painted surfaces. I have been using this technique for years without scratching the shiny black paint on the '32. I never really "wash" the hot rod like I do for our everyday cars.

I have often wondered who might have been the first owner of my 1932 Ford and how they must have enjoyed it. It would have been produced in Detroit, Michigan starting

The Deuce Coupe that Stole My Heart

in March of that year. Ford also had factories in Europe, India, Asia, and Canada producing the new model just after the 1929 stock market crash and ensuing Great Depression. Some people were still working and could afford a new car, but many were not so fortunate with the unemployment rate at 18%. The average wage of a factory worker was probably $4 per day in 1932 and the cost of a new Ford was about $600 depending on the model. So, if you made $1000 a year, a new car was pretty much out of reach. Ford, however, did produced 275,000 cars in 1932, so some people obviously had enough money to purchase one.

If my car spent most of its life in the Minnesota area of the country where it was abandoned in the woods, it probably saw some rough and unimproved road conditions. This would account for why the frame was no longer usable and the body was rusted and rotted on its lower extremities. Who knows how many owners this car had before it was retrieved from the woods and sold to a hot rod company in Nebraska? When I took possession of the '32, I was going to give it a new lease on life. It was a big decision to chop the roof of a car that had spent over eighty years in its original configuration. I wondered if the original owners would cringe at the modification to modernize this classic old car. For me, the decision was easy because I convinced myself that the coupe was too far gone to be restored back to an original full fender configuration. It was the ideal car to become a hot rod in my estimation.

Every time I climb into the '32 to drive it, I still think

back to when it was new and the joy it brought to all those who owned and drove it. It is a sensation that I don't think you could get from a fiberglass body car or a newly minted steel body car. That's why I love this car so much and probably will never sell it. My kids and grandkids can hopefully enjoy the car after I am gone. Maybe they will modify it further with, perhaps, a bigger engine or manual shift transmission. In any event, I hope it brings joy to whoever owns or drives it in the future. At ninety years old as of this writing, the coupe is in better shape than I am at seventy-seven years old! I hope it makes it to 100 years old and beyond.

What great technology we have been introduced to in our lifetime. I'm not so sure fully electric cars are the way to go because it is predicted that the infrastructure to produce enough electricity to charge these vehicles is behind the curve. Battery technology keeps improving but what happens to the discarded batteries in the future? Hopefully, scientists will figure it all out as we progress forward. Maybe hybrid cars are the way to go. Electric, but with a gas engine backup seems more plausible to me. I guess that thinking is just a result of my old-fashioned upbringing and my love of traditional hot rods.

One of my neighbors leased a brand-new Tesla X with gull wing rear doors and all the bells and whistles. I mean, this is a car that can park itself and come to pick you up automatically with just the push of a button.

One day my neighbor gave me the keys to this fabulous new Tesla and said "take it around the block." I accepted the

The Deuce Coupe that Stole My Heart

offer but would only do so with him sitting in the passenger seat. When I stepped on the accelerator, the reaction was immediate. I was surprised at the torque this car had. It was much faster than any car I had driven in the past with a conventional drive train. It was exhilarating to say the least. I really appreciated the offer to drive this new car. It brought me quickly into the twenty first century.

The very next day I drove my 1932 Ford to a local cruise night and realized the vast difference in old versus new technology and how far we have come in my lifetime. I had driven my coupe up to 100 mph one time after I had finished building it, but that same speed in a modern vehicle is hardly noticeable. I can only wonder where technology will take us in the future with fully autonomous vehicles. It's kind of scary, actually. Can you imagine programming a destination into your car's computer and then sitting back and letting it take you there. I'm not quite ready for that yet.

Tesla Model X. The technology in this car is just amazing and the torque during acceleration is probably better than my hot rod.

The Deuce Coupe that Stole My Heart

CHAPTER 21

Over the years I have had the pleasure of meeting some nice people in the car hobby or in business supporting the industry. I traveled to Pomona, California with some friends from the Connecticut Street Rod Association for the 1997 Grand National Roadster Show (GNRS). All the big names in the hot rod business along with amateur car builders and owners show up there to display their creations. The top prize is the selection of Americas Most Beautiful Roadster (AMBR) award. Big names like Chip Foose and Boyd Coddington always win this award. They are professional builders with a lot more money than I have and they can afford the talented mechanics and bodywork people to create these masterpieces.

    I had the pleasure of meeting Boyd Coddington at his shop. A few of us were being escorted around the hot rod shops by good friend Jim Garcia who built my 1930 Ford roadster. At the time of our visit, the TV show *American Hot*

Boyd Coddington, American Hotrod. *A side trip from the Grand National Roadster Show in Pomona, California brought us to this hot rod shop.*

Barry McGuire from the tv show 'Car Crazy'. A real gentleman who featured me and my '32 Ford on a segement of his program.

Rod was being filmed there and video crews were in various areas of the shop. During our tour of the facility a young man who worked there walked up to me and said, "I know you." As it turned out, this young fellow was from Connecticut and dated our niece while she was living with us. He was attending Cheney Technical High School at the time and was taking shop courses in automobile maintenance and sheet metal work. Somehow, he ended up working at the Coddington shop. What a small world it is. Unfortunately, Boyd passed away the following year in 1998.

Back at the GNRS we had the pleasure of meeting Barry Meguiar, president of the car care products company. He had a show on TV for many years by the name of *Car Crazy*. I was lucky enough to be chosen to be on a segment of one of his shows featuring me and my 1932 Ford coupe when it was just in primer. He billed this segment as a non-professional car builder working on his project car, just like many other individuals all around the country. It was my 15 minutes of fame (actually it was only about five minutes). My friend Richard Wickert, who I bought my roadster from, escorted us around the fair grounds.

I met George Barris. He was the builder of the famed Batmobile and had the car on display at this show. He was also responsible for building a number of movie cars such as KITT from *Knight Rider,* The General Lee from the *Dukes of Hazzard,* the Munsters' Koach, and the pickup from the *Beverly Hillbillies,* as well as others. George was an interesting guy and wasn't afraid to think outside the box when it came to his car designs.

LEFT: George Barris of Batmobile fame and creator of a lot of custom cars featured on TV shows and in movies.

RIGHT: Candy Clark, "Debbie" from the movie American Graffiti. *I got a hug and some signed memoribilia from her at the Grand National Roadster Show.*

"Peal out!" was Candy Clark's famous line from the 1973 movie American Graffitti *directed by George Lucas..*

The Deuce Coupe that Stole My Heart

One of my favorite old-time movies was the 1973 film *American Graffiti*. It was a low budget film ($777,000) starring Richard Dreyfuss, Ron Howard, Harrison Ford, Paul LeMat, and Wolfman Jack. The film grossed over $140 million. One of the actresses was Candy Clark who played the blond character, Debbie. She was famous for the line "Peal Out!" in the movie. I met her at the GNRS and had my picture taken with her. She is still good looking. Nice memories.

Big Daddy Don Garlitts with Brenda and me at the museum in Ocala, FL. We took a personalized tour of the facility with a car club group.

Closer to home here in Florida, we have a very famous race car driver nearby in Ocala. Big Daddy Don Garlits was the first drag racer to surpass 170, 180, 200, 240, 250, and 270 miles per hour in the quarter mile. In 2014 at the age of 82, he set a record of 184 miles per hour in a battery powered electric vehicle that he designed and built. The Villages Car Club, to which we belonged at the time. received a personal tour of Don's shop and were treated to the sounds of race car engines that Don started up for us. What an interesting hands-on guy he was during his whole racing career. It takes a lot of guts to drive a dragster 300 miles per hour and Don has the broken body parts to prove it. Besides the shop area, there is a museum of drag racing and a separate museum of antique cars to view. This is a great attraction for car racing enthusiasts.

I have a few neon signs and car related memorabilia displayed in my garage man cave, but they are mostly reproductions. If you ever wondered why you can't find any of the original stuff anymore, it's because it is very costly… and it's all in Don's museums!

Steve VanBlarcom, 3rd from right, with red 200 MPH Club hat. Steve piloted his roadster to set a new record at Bonneville.

The Deuce Coupe that Stole My Heart

Out of the many Connecticut Street Rod Club members that I have known, Steve VanBlarcom stands out and is a truly interesting guy. He has a shop in Wallingford, Connecticut which houses his many hot rods. Not too many years ago in 2009, Steve acquired a 1929 Ford hi-boy roadster that had set a speed record at the Bonneville Salt Flats in Utah. His goal was to break the 209-mph record with that same vehicle. After some trial and error, he eventually set a new record of nearly 217 mph. Other runs on the Salt Flats were clocked at over 220 mph but were not officially counted as a record. Can you imagine traveling at over 200 mph in a 1929 open wheel roadster with 900 horsepower pumping out of a small block Ford engine? What a great accomplishment.

Now I own just one hot rod, my 1932 Ford coupe. I enjoy driving it around our retirement community every once in a while. Sometimes I just hang out in the garage in the evening with a drink and admire my handiwork. I have been instructed by my family to never sell this car because it was a labor of love to build over an eight-year period. The car will more than likely be passed down to my children and maybe eventually even my grandchildren. I still wonder from time to time what a story this car could tell if it could talk about its past ninety years after it came off the assembly line in Detroit in 1932. I'll bet there would be some doozies!

I have had the pleasure of owning many cars during my lifetime. I've had my favorites along the way, but I think the '32 Ford coupe will always be number one. I hope it will still be driven beyond its 100-year anniversary.

Hopefully, younger generations to follow with still appreciate these old cars and hot rods in years to come, even with the introduction of electric vehicles and autonomous vehicles. I think our generation has lived in the best of times. I hope and pray for the same kind of memories for my children and grandchildren.

I hope that you enjoyed my stories. I certainly have enjoyed living them. God bless.

ACKNOWLEDGMENTS

Thank you to my wife, Brenda, who inspires and encourages me to accomplish things that I might not have done on my own.

Thanks to William Mitchell of T*he Villages Daily Sun* for the picture used on the cover of this book.

Thanks to my editor, Wendy Metcalfe, for correcting my grammer, punctuation, and spelling; to John Prince and Hallard Press for guiding me through the book publication process.

Richard Stoebel

OUR CARS OVER THE YEARS

1950 PONTIAC
1960 CHEVROLET CORVAIR
1965 FORD MUSTANG
1960 CORVETTE CONVERTIBLE
1962 VOLKSWAGEN BEETLE
1970 FORD PINTO
1985 FORD THUNDERBIRD
1988 FORD ESCORT
1984 PONTIAC FIERO
1990 LINCOLN MK7
1995 FORD RANGER
2000 FORD F150 STEPSIDE
2004 DODGE RAM 1500

FAMILY OR WIFE'S PERSONAL CARS
1968 PONTIAC FIREBIRD
1970 CHEVROLET MALIBU CLASSIC
1975 FORD F150 VAN
1982 OLDSMOBILE SEDAN
1985 BUICK SEDAN
1990 MAZDA 929
1997 ACURA CL
2000 MERCEDES C SERIES
2007 MERCEDES C SERIES
2011 ACURA RL
2014 CADILLAC SRX
2018 BMW 230i CONVERTIBLE
2022 CADILLAC XT4

ABOUT THE AUTHOR

Richard "Dick" Stoebel spent eight years restoring his '32 Ford five-window coupe into an award-winning hot rod. That was all while helping raise two energetic children, upgrading several new homes, driving boats, piloting airplanes, and working as an engineer on jet engines.

He grew up in a modest New England home, worked during high school, married a beautiful woman, and became an engineer.

While looking back, he also keeps his bucket list solidly in view: fly a helicopter, write a book (check off that one—twice!), cruise the Panama Canal, live to see great grandchildren. He is the author of *I'm Almost History, A Memoir of an American Dream Family* published in 2020.

Now retired in Florida, Dick continues to enjoy the American Dream and can be seen at Cruise Ins and around the squares in his beloved Deuce Coupe.

He hopes that you enjoy reading his book as much as he enjoyed writing it.

www.ingramcontent.com/pod-product-compliance
Lightning Source LLC
Chambersburg PA
CBHW062033120526
44592CB00036B/1988